Valentin Dallmeier

Mining and Checking Object Behavior

Valentin Dallmeier

Mining and Checking Object Behavior

Efficient Mining of Object Behavior Models

Südwestdeutscher Verlag für Hochschulschriften

Impressum/Imprint (nur für Deutschland/ only for Germany)
Bibliografische Information der Deutschen Nationalbibliothek: Die Deutsche Nationalbibliothek verzeichnet diese Publikation in der Deutschen Nationalbibliografie; detaillierte bibliografische Daten sind im Internet über http://dnb.d-nb.de abrufbar.
Alle in diesem Buch genannten Marken und Produktnamen unterliegen warenzeichen-, marken- oder patentrechtlichem Schutz bzw. sind Warenzeichen oder eingetragene Warenzeichen der jeweiligen Inhaber. Die Wiedergabe von Marken, Produktnamen, Gebrauchsnamen, Handelsnamen, Warenbezeichnungen u.s.w. in diesem Werk berechtigt auch ohne besondere Kennzeichnung nicht zu der Annahme, dass solche Namen im Sinne der Warenzeichen- und Markenschutzgesetzgebung als frei zu betrachten wären und daher von jedermann benutzt werden dürften.

Verlag: Südwestdeutscher Verlag für Hochschulschriften GmbH & Co. KG
Dudweiler Landstr. 99, 66123 Saarbrücken, Deutschland
Telefon +49 681 37 20 271-1, Telefax +49 681 37 20 271-0
Email: info@svh-verlag.de
Zugl.: Saarbrücken, Universität des Saarlandes, Dissertation, 2010

Herstellung in Deutschland:
Schaltungsdienst Lange o.H.G., Berlin
Books on Demand GmbH, Norderstedt
Reha GmbH, Saarbrücken
Amazon Distribution GmbH, Leipzig
ISBN: 978-3-8381-2392-9

Imprint (only for USA, GB)
Bibliographic information published by the Deutsche Nationalbibliothek: The Deutsche Nationalbibliothek lists this publication in the Deutsche Nationalbibliografie; detailed bibliographic data are available in the Internet at http://dnb.d-nb.de.
Any brand names and product names mentioned in this book are subject to trademark, brand or patent protection and are trademarks or registered trademarks of their respective holders. The use of brand names, product names, common names, trade names, product descriptions etc. even without a particular marking in this works is in no way to be construed to mean that such names may be regarded as unrestricted in respect of trademark and brand protection legislation and could thus be used by anyone.

Publisher: Südwestdeutscher Verlag für Hochschulschriften GmbH & Co. KG
Dudweiler Landstr. 99, 66123 Saarbrücken, Germany
Phone +49 681 37 20 271-1, Fax +49 681 37 20 271-0
Email: info@svh-verlag.de

Printed in the U.S.A.
Printed in the U.K. by (see last page)
ISBN: 978-3-8381-2392-9

Copyright © 2011 by the author and Südwestdeutscher Verlag für Hochschulschriften GmbH & Co. KG and licensors
All rights reserved. Saarbrücken 2011

Contents

1	**Introduction**	**1**
	1.1 About this Thesis	2
	1.2 Terminology	3
	1.3 Publications	5
2	**Classifying Bugs**	**7**
	2.1 Source Data	7
	2.2 Classification	8
	2.3 Conclusions	10
3	**State of the Art**	**11**
	3.1 Dynamic Program Behavior	11
	3.2 Program Spectra	14
	3.3 Call-Sequence Sets	17
	3.4 Finite State Automata	18
	3.4.1 Learning Finite State Automata	19
	3.4.2 Software Process Models	19
	3.4.3 Extended Finite State Machines	21
	3.4.4 Object Usage Specifications	23
	3.4.5 Markov Chains	24
	3.4.6 Summary	26
	3.5 Invariants	26
	3.6 Conclusions	27
4	**Object Behavior Models**	**29**
	4.1 Identifiers	31
	4.2 Inspectors	32
	4.3 Value Access Paths	32
	4.4 Object States	33
	4.5 Object Behavior Models	34
	4.6 Model Depth	34
	4.7 State Abstraction	38

4.8 Conclusions 39

5 Mining Object Behavior Models   41
5.1 Tracing
41
5.1.1 Data Collection   41
5.1.2 Architecture   43
5.1.3 Principles   44
5.1.4 Traced Data   45
5.1.5 Object Identifiers   47
5.1.6 Tracing Inspector Values   47
5.1.7 Multithreading   48
5.1.8 Runtime Evaluation   48
5.2 Model Mining   49
5.2.1 Dynamic Heap Model   49
5.2.2 Model Generation   51
5.2.3 Runtime Optimizations   52
5.3 Dynamic Side-Effect Analysis   52
5.3.1 Pure Methods   53
5.3.2 Analysis   54
5.3.3 Tracing   54
5.3.4 Algorithm   54
5.3.5 Multiple Program Runs   56
5.3.6 Soundness   56
5.3.7 Evaluation   56
5.3.8 Related Work   60
5.4 Conclusions   61

6 Mining Bug Benchmarks   63
6.1 Motivation   63
6.2 Related Work   65
6.2.1 Existing Benchmark Suites   65
6.2.2 Defect Localization Tools   65
6.2.3 Bug Classification   67
6.3 Bug Extraction from History   67
6.3.1 Prerequisites   67
6.3.2 Fix Identification   68
6.3.3 Extraction   69
6.3.4 Test Execution   69
6.3.5 Associated Tests   70
6.3.6 Meta Information   71
6.3.7 Repository   74

6.4 Subjects 75
    6.4.1 Characteristics 75
    6.4.2 Locality 75
    6.4.3 Size 76
    6.4.4 Syntactical Properties 76
6.5 Minimizing Fixes with Delta Debugging 77
    6.5.1 Delta Debugging 78
    6.5.2 Minimizing Fixes 80
6.6 Biased Data Sets 87
    6.6.1 Bug Features 87
    6.6.2 Results 88
6.7 Conclusions 89

7 Mining Models for Typestate Verification   91
7.1 Typestate Analysis 93
7.2 Mining Typestate Automata 93
7.3 Enriching Typestate Automata 94
7.4 Experimental Evaluation 97
    7.4.1 Subjects 97
    7.4.2 Quantitative Evaluation 99
    7.4.3 Qualitative Evaluation 100
    7.4.4 Usefulness 103
    7.4.5 Threats to Validity 106
7.5 Related Work 107
    7.5.1 Test Case Generation 107
    7.5.2 Typestate Verification 108
    7.5.3 Specification Mining 108
7.6 Conclusions 109

8 Generating Fixes from Object Behavior Anomalies   111
8.1 Mining Models 114
    8.1.1 Mining Preconditions 115
8.2 Detecting Violations 116
8.3 Generating Fixes 118
    8.3.1 Inserting Calls 118
    8.3.2 Deleting Calls 118
8.4 Choosing the Best Fix 119
8.5 Experimental Evaluation 119
    8.5.1 Subjects 119
    8.5.2 Experimental Setup 120
    8.5.3 Running the Experiments 120

CONTENTS

	8.5.4	Performance	121
	8.5.5	Results	121
	8.5.6	Discussion	127
	8.5.7	Threats to Validity	128
8.6		Applicability	129
8.7		Related Work	130
	8.7.1	Locating Bugs	130
	8.7.2	Repairing Programs	131
	8.7.3	Leveraging Specifications	131
	8.7.4	Repairing State	131
	8.7.5	Mining Specifications	132
	8.7.6	Generating Tests	132
8.8		Conclusions	132

9 Conclusions and Future Work — 133
- 9.1 iBugs — 134
- 9.2 Tautoko — 135
- 9.3 Pachika — 135

A Additional Figures and Tables — 137

B Trace File Format Description — 145
- B.1 Concepts — 145
  - B.1.1 Serialization — 146
  - B.1.2 Object Identifiers — 146
  - B.1.3 Method Identifiers — 146
  - B.1.4 Field Identifiers — 146
  - B.1.5 Thread Identifiers — 146
  - B.1.6 Allocation Site Identifiers — 146
  - B.1.7 Invocation Site Identifiers — 146
- B.2 Events — 147
  - B.2.1 Identifier Events — 147
  - B.2.2 Method Call Events — 149
  - B.2.3 Parameter Events — 150
  - B.2.4 Return Events — 150
  - B.2.5 Field Access Events — 151
  - B.2.6 Array Access Events — 152
  - B.2.7 Inspector Events — 152
  - B.2.8 List of Event Identifiers — 153

Bibliography — 155

List of Figures

1.1	The first computer bug.	4
2.1	Syntactical properties of bugs in Eclipse.	9
3.1	A generic execution model.	12
3.2	Different program spectra for gcd.	16
3.3	Call-sequence set abstraction.	17
3.4	Over-generalizing automata.	20
3.5	Automaton generated by the k-tail algorithm.	21
3.6	Example of an extended finite state machine.	22
3.7	An object usage specification for Iterator.	22
3.8	Branch-based Markov model.	25
4.1	An object behavior model for the Vector class.	30
4.2	Uml schema for a car management application.	33
4.3	An object behavior model for the IMAPProtocol class.	35
4.4	An object behavior model for Vector.	36
4.5	A model for PersistenceManager.	37
5.1	Overview of Adabu.	42
5.2	Architecture of the tracing framework.	44
5.3	Example instrumentation for a field write operation.	45
5.4	Stack manipulation step by step.	46
5.5	An example of a dynamic heap.	50
5.6	Examples of pure methods.	53
5.7	Purity results for AspectJ.	57
6.1	Linking bug reports and changes.	69
6.2	Pre- and post-fix versions for a bug.	70
6.3	Building and testing pre-fix and post-fix versions.	71
6.4	Comparison of pre-fix and post-fix versions.	73
6.5	Fingerprints for Bug 87376.	74
6.6	Histogram for fixes in AspectJ and Rhino.	76
6.7	Sizes of fixes for AspectJ and Rhino.	77

LIST OF FIGURES

6.8	Example fix for bug 203402.	86
7.1	Overview of Tautoko.	92
7.2	Typestate for SMTPProtocol.	93
7.3	Initial model of the SMTPProtocol class.	95
7.4	Enriched model of the SMTPProtocol class.	96
7.5	Evaluation scheme for Tautoko.	102
7.6	A screenshot of the Eclipse integration for JFTA.	110
8.1	Combined model for the BaseIOAcceptor class.	112
8.2	Overview of how Pachika works.	113
8.3	A deep model for PersistenceManager.	115
8.4	Fix generated by Pachika for bug 173602.	125
8.5	Fix generated by Pachika for bug 121616.	125
8.6	Fix generated by Pachika for bug 51322.	126
8.7	Fix generated by Pachika for bug 60015.	127
A.1	Step-by-step guide to iBUGS (1/2).	138
A.2	Step-by-step guide to iBUGS (2/2).	139
A.3	Examples for different bugs with fingerprints (1/3).	140
A.4	Examples for different bugs with fingerprints (2/3).	141
A.5	Examples for different bugs with fingerprints (3/3).	142
A.6	Repository entry for bug 69459.	143

List of Tables

2.1	Manual classification of bugs.	8
3.1	Tracing results for the Spec benchmarks.	15
3.2	A subset of invariant types provided by Daikon.	27
4.1	Invariant templates used by abstraction function.	39
5.1	Runtime overhead of Adabu.	49
5.2	Runtime overhead of JPure.	60
6.1	Overview of evaluation methods for bug localization tools.	66
6.2	Bug candidates analyzed for AspectJ.	68
6.3	Token types in Apfel.	73
6.4	Statistics of the development history of AspectJ and Rhino.	75
6.5	Number of bugs per fingerprint in AspectJ and Rhino.	78
6.6	Minimization results for Rhino.	82
6.7	Minimization results for AspectJ (1/2).	83
6.8	Minimization results for AspectJ (2/2).	84
6.9	Subjects used in the evaluation of bug bias.	89
7.1	Subjects of the Tautoko case study.	97
7.2	Quantitative results for Tautoko.	100
7.3	Statistics of manually specified models.	100
7.4	Sources of test runs for Tautoko.	104
7.5	Evaluation of true positives for Tautoko.	105
7.6	Evaluation of false positives for Tautoko.	106
8.1	Subjects used in the evaluation of Pachika.	120
8.2	Runtime overhead of Pachika.	121
8.3	Evaluation results for crashing bugs in AspectJ.	122
8.4	Evaluation results for non-crashing bugs in AspectJ.	123
8.5	Evaluation results for bugs in Rhino.	124
8.6	Overview of classes with preconditions.	130
B.1	Event identifiers processed by Adabu.	154

Chapter 1

Introduction

According to a study in 2002 by the National Institute of Standards and Technology (NIST), software errors cost the economy of the United States "an estimated $59.5 billion annually" [79], which amounts to 0.6 percent of the gross national product of the United States in 2002. Obviously, software errors (also referred to as bugs) and their effects are a serious problem for the economy. Almost eight years have passed since the NIST study was published. Have things improved since then?

In the last few years, we have witnessed several bugs in widely-used systems. In January 2009, Microsoft's Zune player stopped working due to a bug in the date calculation library. Millions of users were unable to use their Zune for a few days. Not being able to listen to music admittedly is no life-threatening problem. However, one year later, millions of clients of easycash (a large electronic cash provider) were unable to use their cards for a few weeks. Again, there was a bug in the date calculation library. In that case, the effects of the bug were more severe. Customers were unable to shop, and thousands of ATMs had to be re-programmed, causing costs of millions of Euros. Obviously, bugs are still a problem and the effects are getting worse as more people rely on software-based systems. Hence, the need for solutions that help avoid bugs or limit their effects is strong.

Researchers have long since recognized this problem and are developing approaches to solve it. A broad range of techniques tries to *prevent bugs* from occurring: The EROSE tool [123] leverages historical information to remind a developer of missing changes. New programming languages such as JAVA make whole classes of errors obsolete, and new programming paradigms such as Extreme Programming introduce new ways to develop software. However, as the Zune and easycash examples show, software still contains bugs and hence we also need techniques that help us *debug* a program.

Researchers have proposed a number of approaches that try to automatically *localize bugs*. For example, the TARANTULA tool ranks statements according to execution profiles from passing and failing runs. A statement that is executed often in the failing run, but seldom or never in passing runs is likely to be the cause for the problem and is therefore ranked at the top. TARANTULA is an example of a class of techniques that are based on comparing the behavior of programs across different runs. Many of these approaches compare the behavior of a *failing run* that exhibits a problem to one or more *passing runs* where the program behaves correctly. By analyzing differences in the behavior, these approaches identify statements that are likely to be the cause for the failure. The key feature of such behavior-based approaches is the way program behavior is modeled. Existing techniques range from simple statistical models [52, 57, 92, 29] to sophisticated techniques that model program behavior as dynamic invariants [39].

In this thesis, we present a novel approach to modeling program behavior. In contrast to existing approaches, our technique is specifically targeted at *object-oriented languages*. In the object-oriented world, code and variables that are concerned with implementing an entity are grouped together in *objects*. Our approach mines so-called *object behavior models* that describe the behavior of individual objects at runtime. Such models come in the form of finite state automata, where states correspond to different states of the object, and transitions occur due to method invocations. To learn these models, we observe example executions of the program as provided by the program's test suite. When learned from correct examples, an object behavior model describes the correct usage of a class. In this thesis, we investigate two different approaches that use object behavior models as a specification of correct usage, and to compare the behavior of objects across different program runs:

Preventing Bugs We learn behavior models by tracing the regression test suite of a library and use existing *static analysis* techniques to find incorrect API usage already when code is developed. Our approach is implemented as an ECLIPSE plugin that highlights incorrect usage whenever the developer changes code.

Fixing Bugs We present an approach that generates fixes for failing runs. Our technique compares object behavior models from passing and failing runs, and generates fix candidates based on differences in the models. Evaluated on a set of realistic projects, our tool was able to generate fixes for a number of real-life bugs.

To judge the effectiveness of these techniques, we would like to evaluate their performance on a set of real-life bugs. Unfortunately, existing bug repositories such as the Software-Artifact Infrastructure Repository (SIR) [37] provide mostly small subjects with artificially seeded bugs. An evaluation based on subjects from this repository would be flawed, because the results can hardly be generalized to realistic programs. To avoid these problems, we have developed a new approach to mining bug benchmarks from a project's development history. The result of our efforts is a publicly available repository called IBUGS that contains over 300 bugs mined from the history of two large open-source projects.

1.1 About this Thesis

The most important contribution of this thesis is an approach to mine models of object behavior for programs with realistic size and an evaluation of two approaches that use these models to solve real-world problems. A lot of effort went into making our tools scale to real-world programs and to empirically validate the usefulness of our techniques. All tools and data sets developed in the course of our work are publicly available. This will hopefully encourage other researchers to further explore the approaches presented in this thesis and to find new applications for object behavior models. The remainder of this thesis is structured as follows:

- In Chapter 2, we pave the road for the work presented in subsequent chapters by analyzing structural properties of a large number of fixes. Our findings show that many bug fixes are small and touch only few lines in a single method.

- In Chapter 3, we present the state of the art in software execution models. We provide a classification of approaches based on the types of information used, and discuss advantages and disadvantages of each approach.

- In Chapter 4, we introduce object behavior models as a novel way of representing program behavior. We give a formal definition and present advantages and disadvantages of our technique.

- In Chapter 5, we present ADABU, a tool that mines object behavior models from the execution of JAVA programs. We highlight important technical aspects of the tool, and present lessons learned for implementing dynamic program analysis techniques in JAVA.

- In Chapter 6, we present the IBUGS approach, which mines real bugs from version archives and bug databases. Based on our technique, we have created a repository of programs with real bugs. This repository is publicly available and can be used to compare the performance of approaches that are concerned with bugs and their effects.

- In Chapter 7, we use object behavior models as input for typestate verification, a static analysis that detects misuses of classes. Since most test suites do not trigger exceptions, our tool called TAUTOKO mutates the test suite in order to *enrich* the initial specification. Evaluated on a set of seeded bugs, a typestate verifier that uses enriched specifications finds significantly more bugs that when using the initial specification.

- In Chapter 8, we present PACHIKA, a tool that generates fixes for bugs based on differences in object behavior models mined from passing and failing runs.

The thesis concludes with a summary and ideas for future work in Chapter 9. The remainder of this chapter defines common terms used throughout the thesis, and lists publications related to this thesis.

1.2 Terminology

A widely accepted model for software failures was developed by Zeller [119]. When working with a program, we sometimes observe incorrect behavior: The program crashes or produces incorrect output. In this case, we say that the program *fails* or that we can observe a *failure*. An example for such a failure that occurred often in the early days of the Windows operating system is the famous blue screen: All of a sudden, Windows displayed a white error message on blue background and completely stopped working. A program run that exhibits no failure is referred to as a *passing run*. Accordingly, a run that shows a failure is called a *failing run*.

Zeller identifies four different stages of how a failure comes to be:

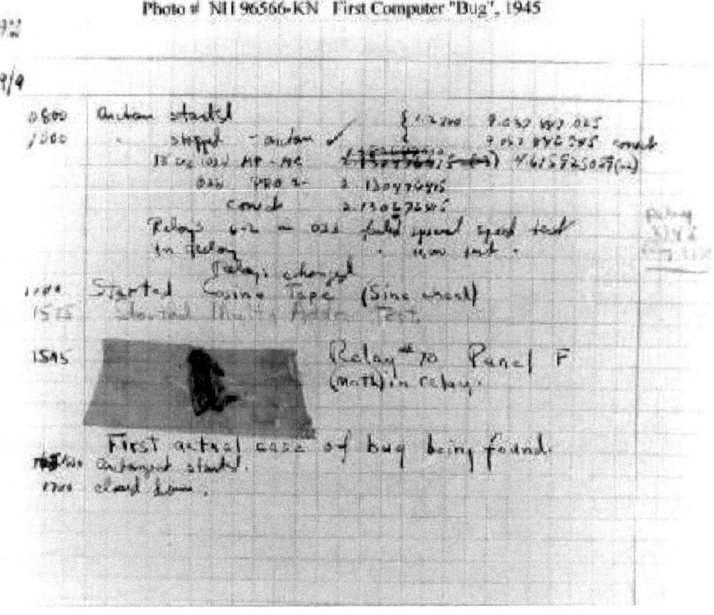

Figure 1.1: The first computer bug. In 1945, scientists working at the Mark II computer at Harvard University found a dead moth in one of the components. This soon became known as the "first actual case of bug being found".

- At the beginning, the programmer introduces a *defect* (or *bug*) in the program. A defect is a piece of code that causes an infection of the program state (see below). In other words, a defect is the piece of code that is responsible for the failure.

- When the defective code is executed, it creates an *infection* of the program state. After the defect is executed the program state differs from what the programmer had in mind.

- As the execution continues, the infection is further propagated through the program state. Functions that take already infected program state as input may cause the infection to spread through the program state.

- Finally, the infection causes the *failure*. For example, the infection may violate conditions that are necessary for the invocation of a function. Such violations may result in null pointer dereferences, or in failed assertions. At this point, the problem becomes visible to the user.

As soon as the developer observes a failure, he has to *debug* the program. Debugging requires to analyze the infection chain, find the root of the infection (the defect) and remove it such that the failure no longer occurs and the program behaves correctly.

1.3 Publications

This thesis builds on the following papers (in chronological order):

- **Valentin Dallmeier**, Christian Lindig, Andrzej Wasylkowski, Andreas Zeller. Mining object behavior with ADABU. In *WODA '06: Proceedings of the 2006 International Workshop on Dynamic Systems Analysis*, pages 17–24, New York, NY, USA, 2006. ACM.

- **Valentin Dallmeier** and Thomas Zimmermann. Extraction of bug localization benchmarks from history. In *ASE '07: Proceedings of the twenty-second IEEE/ACM International Conference on Automated Software Engineering*, pages 433–436, New York, NY, USA, 2007. ACM.

- **Valentin Dallmeier**, Andreas Zeller, and Bertrand Meyer. Generating fixes from object behavior anomalies. *ASE '09: Proceedings of the twenty-fourth IEEE/ACM International Conference on Automated Software Engineering*, pages 550–554, 2009.

- **Valentin Dallmeier**, Nikolai Knopp, Christoph Mallon, Sebastian Hack, and Andreas Zeller. Generating test cases for specification mining. In *ISSTA '10: Proceedings of the 19th International Symposium on Software testing and analysis* (New York, NY, USA, 2010), ACM, pp. 85–96.

Chapter 2

Classifying Bugs

In this thesis, we are concerned with finding new approaches related to bugs in programs. Before developing our approach, we first perform a *syntactical analysis* of a large number of real bugs and attempt to find a classification that covers as many bugs as possible. Such a classification would provide us with insights on the structure of bugs, and would also allow us to direct our work towards large bug classes.

In this chapter, we present an analysis of the bugs recorded for the ECLIPSE project[1], which provides an open-source development environment for JAVA. We first try to automatically classify bugs based on a comparison of the program right before and right after a bug was fixed. After that, we manually verify the results of the automatic classification. Our results show that even when manually analyzing each bug, it is difficult to provide a precise classification for the majority of bugs.

In the remainder of this chapter, we present details of the data used in the study (Section 2.1), present the results of our experiment (Section 2.2), and discuss our findings (Section 2.3). Parts of this study were carried out by Markus Thiele in his bachelor's thesis [102].

2.1 Source Data

To perform our experiment, we use the APFEL [122] tool to extract data from the version archives and bug databases of ECLIPSE. APFEL represents source code as *sets of tokens* extracted from the abstract syntax tree. By comparing token sets of versions right before and after a bug was fixed, we are able to characterize the changes that comprise a bug fix.

For our study, we have used APFEL to process all files and bug reports of ECLIPSE filed before the end of May 2006. APFEL links bug reports to code changes by analyzing commit messages for keywords and bug identifiers. We leverage this linking to identify versions and analyze token sets of changes that fix bugs.

Altogether, the database contains 24 300 bugs that can be associated with code changes. Figure 2.1 shows the size distribution of all changes in terms of the number of affected files, classes, methods and lines. For all features, the distribution is roughly exponential, indicating that the typical bug is small and affects only few lines of code that are usually located in a single method. The size of the

---
[1] http://www.eclipse.org

Bug Class	Percentage
Missing or Faulty Null Check	19.09
Faulty Boolean Expression	8.50
Faulty Arithmetic Expression	1.38
Faulty Comparison	1.21
Lacking Exception Handling	1.08
Lacking Thread Synchronization	0.16
Lacking Initialization	0.45
Unclassified	68.13

Table 2.1: Results of the manual classification of bugs. The largest class of bugs is concerned with null pointer dereferences. Two thirds of the bugs cannot be classified.

fixes ranges from a single line to huge changes affecting several thousand methods. Since classifying such complex changes is difficult, we chose to include only fixes that touch at most six lines in a single method. Altogether, we found 2478 such fixes.

2.2 Classification

Once the dataset was fixed, we collected a catalog of potential bug classes. To that end, we analyzed the types of bugs found by existing bug finding tools such as FINDBUGS [54]. The resulting catalog contains seven classes of bugs, which are intentionally kept abstract to capture larger classes of bugs and to facilitate the analysis. Each class maps to a certain set of tokens as extracted by APFEL, which allowed for an easy classification.

Unfortunately, automatic classification based on APFEL turned out to be too imprecise. In many cases, fixes were classified wrong due to changes unrelated to fixing the bug. To overcome this problem, we complemented the automatic classification by manually verifying all classified fixes. The results of the manual verification are summarized in Table 2.1. It shows the bug classes and the percentage of bugs in each class. The table shows that about two thirds of all classifications are wrong or just coincidental. Coincidental classifications are mostly due to the nature of the data generated by APFEL, which sometimes provides a too coarse abstraction over the data in the syntax tree.

Among those bugs that were classified, we were able to identify two classes that occur relatively often in practice. Missing or wrong null checks account for almost 20% of all bugs. Missing checks are often related to variables whose value is obtained by calling another method, indicating that developers often make wrong assumptions about the postconditions of other methods. Another large class of bugs is due to errors in boolean and arithmetical expressions. One reason why these expressions are often wrong is that they are usually more complex than for example simple method calls, and therefore provide more potential for errors.

2.2. CLASSIFICATION

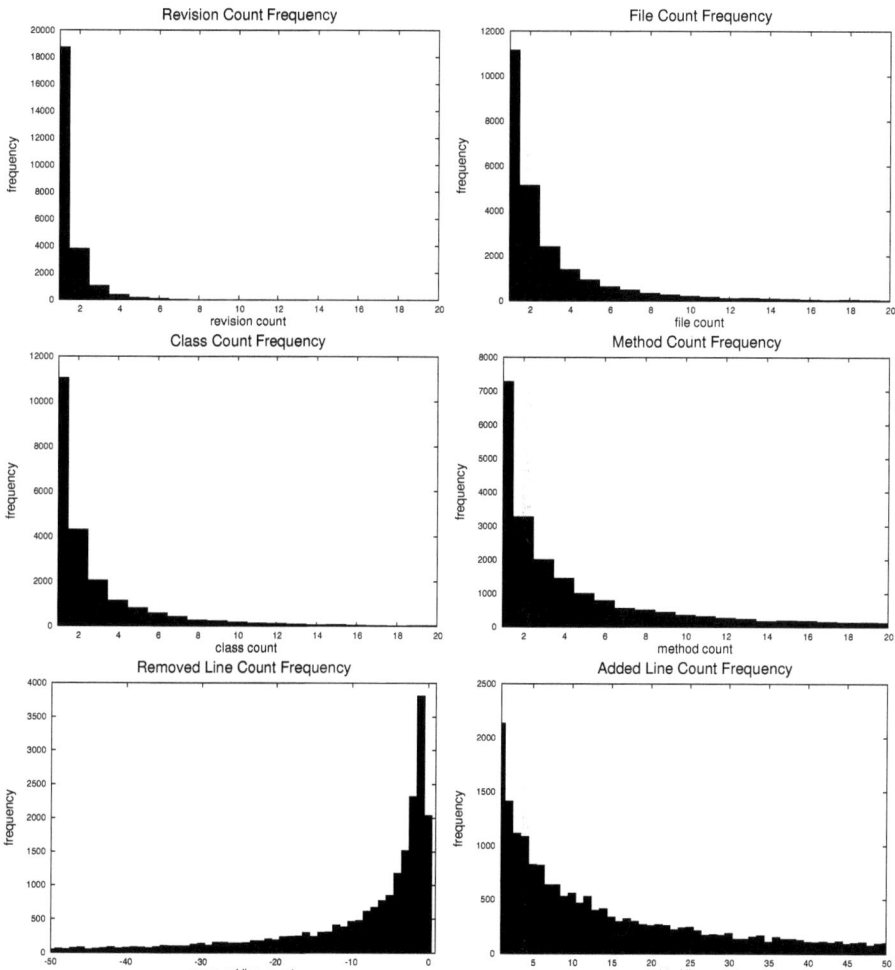

Figure 2.1: Syntactical properties of bugs reported for the ECLIPSE development environment. For all size properties, the distribution is exponential, indicating that the typical fix is small.

2.3 Conclusions

There are two important conclusions we can draw from the above study. First, the typical bug fix is small and affects only a small number of methods. We suspect that this is at least partly due to the fact that we are dealing with post-release bugs, where the program usually works and only seldom shows erroneous behavior. Thus, a bug often requires only a small change, since the functionality is already implemented and to a large part tested. This gives rise to the hope that it may actually be feasible to synthesize fixes, at least for a small class of bugs. In Chapter 8, we investigate such an approach and show that automatically generating fixes is actually possible.

Our second conclusion is based on our failure to classify over two thirds of the bugs in the study. Obviously, despite the small size, most bug fixes are too complex to be expressed in terms of static information such as tokens from an abstract syntax tree. To be able to capture more complex bugs, we need more information, and possibly also a better formalism to represent the information. One way to obtain more information about a program is to execute it and gather information while the program runs. As our experiments in the next chapter will show, observing an execution yields gigabytes of data, and the challenge for any approach to modeling program behavior is therefore find a good abstraction over all this data that captures the essence of the program run.

Chapter 3

State of the Art

Once a developer has finished implementing a program, he needs to *test* the correctness of the implementation. To test a program, it is usually executed several times with different inputs. If the program crashes or the observed output is incorrect, the developer knows that the program contains a *bug*. To solve this problem, the developer needs to *debug* the program, that is he needs to locate and fix the bug in the source code.

One way to debug a program is to execute it and investigate each step of the execution. Inside his head, the developer creates a *mental model* of the program and its behavior. By comparing the model against a specification of the intended behavior, the developer is able to find locations where the observed behavior first deviates from the intended behavior. Assuming that the model is accurate and the specification correct, these locations contain bugs. Depending on the complexity of the program, locating a bug may take days or even weeks.

This thesis investigates the use of *software execution models* to help the programmer in various debugging related activities. A software execution model captures the behavior of a program in a model that can be processed automatically. Thus we can hopefully reduce the manual effort that is related to debugging.

There are a number of existing approaches that mine varying forms of software execution models. In general, the biggest challenge when developing a model is to find the right level of abstraction to use. In this Chapter, we investigate the state of the art in software execution models. To approach the problem, we first introduce a notion of what constitutes dynamic program behavior (Section 3.1). Starting from a generic execution model, we discuss what kinds of information are available at runtime, and present an experiment that investigates how much data is accumulated when observing all aspects of an execution. Observations from this experiment form the starting point for a survey of existing software execution models presented in the remainder of the chapter.

3.1 Dynamic Program Behavior

What information can we observe when executing a program? To answer this question, we first need to devise a model for the execution of a program. As there are many different programming languages and platforms upon which programs are run, such a model has to be very abstract to be valid for a

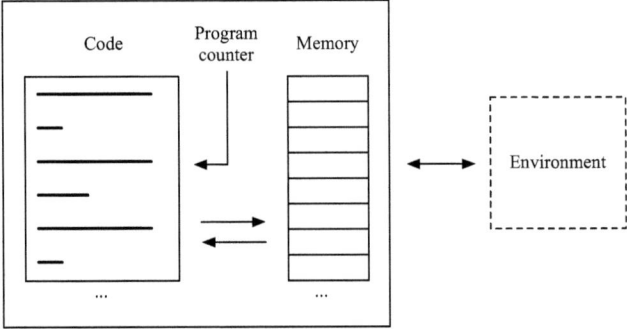

Figure 3.1: A generic execution model. The program consists of individual instructions which alter memory and update the program counter. The environment encompasses all external resources.

broad range of configurations. Figure 3.1 shows a generic execution model that consists of four different parts:

Code This is the actual code of the program that is to be run. It consists of a list of instructions (machine code, virtual machine instructions) that are executed individually. Each instruction is identified by its address.

Program Counter The program counter (pc) is a special variable that stores the address of the next instruction to execute.

Memory At runtime, data is stored in memory, which is organized in individual cells that hold the values of variables or constants. In general, an instruction can read or write the contents of individual cells.

Environment The environment summarizes all external resources that are accessible during the execution. Examples for external resources are files and network connections.

After initialization, execution of a program proceeds as follows: First, the instruction referenced by the pc is loaded. After that, the instruction is executed, possibly altering memory cells. Finally, the pc is updated with the next instruction to execute. At first glance, it may seem unnecessary to distinguish the program counter from the rest of the memory. However, in contrast to all other cells, the pc has a predefined semantics that is vital for the execution of the program.

Given the above model, what information can we record for the individual parts?

Code For this thesis, we assume that the code does not change over time[1]. Hence, the set of instructions is already known at program start and we do not need to record it.

---

[1] Many applications (e.g. RHINO [78], an interpreter for JAVASCRIPT) written in modern languages use dynamically generated code. For such applications it might be interesting to also trace changes to the code.

3.1. DYNAMIC PROGRAM BEHAVIOR

Program Counter The program counter is the part that changes most often in the course of the execution. Its values over time capture the order in which instructions are executed. This information, which we refer to as the *control-flow* of the execution, is a vital part of the program's runtime behavior. To capture control-flow, we need to record the *pc* after the execution of every instruction.

Memory When the program executes, it uses the memory to store information. Individual cells may hold interim results of an algorithm or values that affect the control-flow of the program. The state of the memory over time is therefore also an essential part of the program's runtime behavior. For the remainder of this thesis, we will use the term *memory state* to refer to the state of all memory cells. When tracing memory state, we record all changes to memory cells.

Environment Capturing the environment, although theoretically possible, is difficult in practice. For example, if the program uses a network link to communicate with a server, there is no way to access the state of the other machine. Thus, for this thesis, we do not trace the program's environment. However, we do not expect this to be much of a problem, as those parts of the environment that are important for the behavior of the program will eventually be stored in memory and thus become part of the memory state.

For this thesis, we consider dynamic program behavior to consist of control- and memory state information as defined above. Depending on the application, the amount to which each type is recorded can vary. For example, an application may only be interested in specific parts of the memory, and thus records only changes to those parts. How can we record dynamic behavior in a way that is flexible enough to support the needs of different applications? In this regard, we follow existing approaches and record a *trace of events* that are interesting for the application. For example, an event may be the execution of an instruction that changes the value of a memory cell. We refer to such traces as *execution traces*:

Definition 1 (Execution Trace) *An execution trace s is a sequence* $s = <(t_1,d_1), (t_2,d_2),\ldots,(t_n,d_n)>$ *of trace entries* (t_i,d_i) *where d_i denotes the data that is recorded for the entry, and t_i denotes the time stamp of the entry* $(t_{i-1} < t_i < t_{i+1})$.

This definition is intentionally very generic, since existing approaches require different kinds of data. Depending on the application, a single trace may contain entries with both control-flow and memory state information. For example, the program spectra approach (Section 3.2) traces only control-flow information, whereas the DAIKON tool (Section 3.5) traces a mixture of control-flow and memory state information.

Even short program runs execute millions of instructions and update memory millions of times. Is it actually feasible to trace all this information, and if so, how much data is accumulated? To answer these questions, we have used the tracer of the ADABU tool (see Chapter 5) to trace all control-flow and memory state information available when executing a JAVA program. As a subject for our investigation, we have used a subset of the programs in the SPEC JAVA virtual machine benchmark suite, which contains a set of programs used to test the performance of virtual machines. To collect the data, we ran the tracer with different configurations and analyzed the sizes of the generated traces.

Table 3.1 summarizes the results of the experiment: The first column lists the benchmark name, the second column gives the execution time of the original program run measured as CPU seconds. The remaining two columns list the sizes of the trace files for tracing only control-flow (column three), as well as tracing both memory state and control-flow (column four).

Trace Size On average, a program run generates over 19 gigabytes of trace data per second. This is a very large number, especially when compared to the relatively small sizes of the programs and their input data (the whole benchmark with input data has less than 100 megabytes). The huge amount of data makes it difficult to capture and analyze the whole execution.

Control-Flow vs. Memory State Tracing only the control-flow reduces the amount of data produced to roughly one third. At first glance, this seems surprising since there is only one program counter but there can easily be hundreds of variables. This is due to the fact that the trace only records changes of values. Changing the value of a variable requires to execute an instruction, which in turn causes a change to the program counter. Thus, for every change to a variable we also record one change to the program counter.

To summarize, tracing control-flow and memory state for the whole execution is possible, however it generates gigabytes of data. The sheer size of the trace file makes it difficult to handle the data, and comparing runs based on such large amounts of data is even more difficult.

In the remainder of this chapter, we present an overview of existing software execution models that apply different abstraction techniques to reduce the amount of information: *Program spectra* (Section 3.2) and *call-sequence sets* (Section 3.3) count how often certain features of the control-flow such as executed statements or sequences of method calls can be observed. Section 3.4 presents a number of approaches that encode dynamic behavior using *finite state automata*. The presented approaches range from grammar inference techniques (Section 3.4.2) to probabilistic models (Section 3.4.5). We conclude our survey with DAIKON (Section 3.5), one of the few approaches that focus on the values of variables rather than on control-flow.

3.2 Program Spectra

Early approaches to capture dynamic program behavior focused on finding performance bottlenecks in applications. To that end, these approaches record execution times for code blocks on different levels of granularity. The first approach that went beyond simple timing analysis is the work by Reps et al. [87], which gave rise to a series of other publications [52, 57, 92] that use the same underlying idea. Reps et al. introduced *program spectra*, a statistical approach that records how often a certain characteristic is observed in a run.

Definition 2 (Counting Spectrum) *A counting spectrum of a run consists of a mapping of features to the number of times the feature was observed in the run.*

3.2. PROGRAM SPECTRA

Benchmark	Runtime (Seconds)	Trace Sizes	
		Control-Flow (Gigabytes)	Memory + Control-Flow (Gigabytes)
compress	3.2	23.1	75.2
crypto.rsa	3.6	16.2	35.8
crypto.signverify	2.6	4.3	11.2
scimark.fft	1.1	7.9	23.2
scimark.lu	1.9	13.2	55.2
scimark.monte_carlo	5.0	41.1	146.1
scimark.sor	2.0	4.5	35.3
scimark.sparse	2.6	18.2	51.6

Table 3.1: Trace sizes and execution times for the compress, crypto, and scimark benchmarks in SPECJVM2008.

Most spectra use control-flow information as features. For example, a *counting path spectrum* counts the number of times each loop-free path through the control-flow graph was executed in a run. In their work, Reps et al. use counting path spectra to identify paths in the program along which the control-flow diverges. The goal of this work was to automatically identify parts of the code that were affected by date calculations, and hence might be affected by the y2k problem. To achieve this goal, Reps et al. compare counting path spectra of runs where the supplied inputs are the same except for the dates. In an evaluation, the approach reliably identified a large portion of the relevant code sections.

Besides counting spectra, another type of program spectra used in many applications is called *binary spectra*.

Definition 3 (Binary Spectrum) *A binary spectrum is a counting spectrum that only distinguishes counts equal to and larger than zero.*

A popular binary spectrum is *statement coverage*, which records the set of statements that were executed at least once in a run. Besides control-flow paths and statements, there are a number of other features used for spectra:

Execution-trace spectra record the sequence of statements traversed in a program run. The main conceptual difference to path spectra is that this type also reflects how often loops in the program are executed. Execution-trace spectra are usually much larger than path spectra.

Branch spectra record the set of conditional branches that are traversed in a run. The spectrum is either binary (that is, a branch was hit or not) or includes counts for each time a branch was hit. Compared to path spectra, this spectrum does not record whole paths but instead only counts how often branches in the control-flow graph are visited.

	Statements	Branches	def-use-pairs	
`int gcd(int a,`	1		(a,1,5)	✔
`         int b){`	2		(b,2,5)	✔
`  int r;`	3		(r,5,6)	✔
`  do {`	4		(r,5,8)	
`    r = a % b;`	5	✔	(b,2,7)	
`    if (r > 0){`	6	✔ 6,true	(b,8,7)	
`      a = b;`	7	6,false ✔	(r,5,10)	✔
`      b = r;`	8		(b,8,11)	✔
`    }`	9		(a,7,5)	
`  } while (r > 0);`	10	✔ 10,true	(b,8,5)	
`  return b;`	11	✔ 10,false ✔	(b,2,11)	
`}`	12			

Figure 3.2: Statement, branch and definition-use spectra for a run of the `gcd` method with input (6,3).

Data-dependence spectra count how often a definition-use pair was traversed. A definition-use pair consists of a defining statement (usually an assignment to a variable) and a use statement (read access to the previously stored value from the same variable). This spectrum captures how the execution follows data dependencies in the program.

Figure 3.2 shows an example that illustrates the aforementioned types of spectra. On the left side, the figure shows the code of a method to calculate the greatest common denominator of two integers. The columns to the right show the binary statement, branch and definition-use-pairs spectra obtained when invoking `gcd` with (6,3).

The dominant application for program spectra is *bug localization*. A spectra-based bug localization tool requires a failing and one or more passing runs to analyze differences in failing and passing spectra. The hypothesis is that these differences point to locations in the source code that are likely to contain the bug. Harrold and colleagues [52] were the first to investigate this hypothesis for path and branch spectra. Their work was later refined in the TARANTULA [57] tool which uses statement spectra to find potentially buggy statements. Most recently, Santelices and colleagues [92] have used a combination of statement, branch and definition-use pair spectra to further improve the accurateness of fault localization using spectra.

To summarize, spectra are a concise way of representing a program run. By using different features, spectra capture different aspects of the execution. Existing spectra-based approaches mostly use control-flow features, as the range of values is usually limited (for example, the number of different statements in a program usually is much smaller than the range of different values a single numerical variable can have).

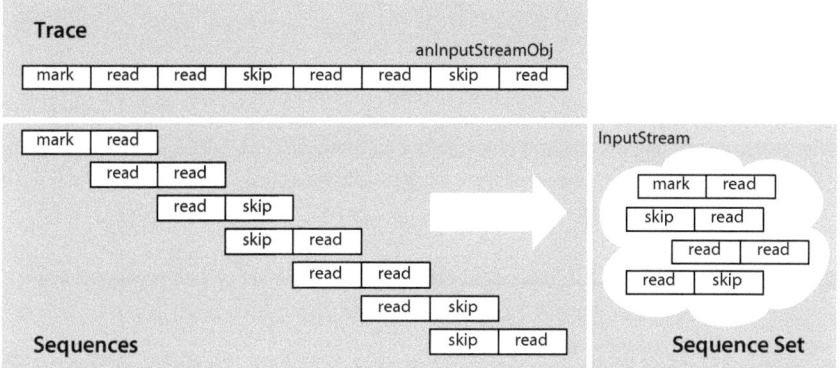

Figure 3.3: Traces are abstracted into call-sequence sets by sliding a window of fixed length over the trace. The call-sequence set contains all distinct observed window contents.

3.3 Call-Sequence Sets

One drawback of many types of spectra is that they disregard the temporal ordering of events in the execution trace. As a consequence, such spectra cannot detect bugs that solely affect the order of execution. In previous work [29], we have devised an execution model called *call-sequence sets* that is specifically targeted at capturing the order of events in a run. In short, the approach works by observing the sequence of method calls issued by each object in isolation. The resulting per-object traces are abstracted to call-sequence sets by sliding a window of length k over the trace. The whole process is illustrated in Figure 3.3.

Definition 4 (Call-Sequence Set Trace) *A trace for capturing call-sequence sets contains one entry for every method invocation observed. A trace entry (t_n, d_n) contains data $d_n = m_n, o_n$ where m_n is an identifier for the method and o_n is an identifier for the object the method was invoked on.*

Using object identifiers, the single call-sequence set trace is demultiplexed into one trace per object. We group trace entries based on the *caller* of the invoked method[2], thus capturing the *behavior of objects*. Unfortunately, the resulting per-object traces are still very large and difficult to compare. To reduce the amount of data to be processed, we abstract the per-object traces into call-sequence sets as follows:

Definition 5 (Call-Sequence Set) *For a given trace s of method calls and a window size k, the set of call-sequences of length k $C(s,k)$ is the set of k-long sub strings of s: $C(s,k) = \{w \mid w \text{ is a sub string of } s \land |w| = k\}$.*

---
[2]In the paper [29], this is referred to as *outgoing* method calls.

Example 1 (Call-Sequence Set) *For a trace* $s = <a,b,c,a,b,c,d,c>$ *and a window size* $k = 2$ *slid over s, the call-sequence set* $C(s,2)$ *is*

$$C(s,2) = \{\langle a,b \rangle, \langle b,c \rangle, \langle c,a \rangle, \langle c,d \rangle, \langle d,c \rangle\}$$

Obviously, abstracting an execution trace into a call-sequence set entails a loss of information. The amount of temporal information retained in the call-sequence set is controlled by the window size k. For larger values of k, the resulting set is larger and contains more information.

Example 2 (Equivalence of Call-Sequence Sets) *For* $k = 2$, *the set of call-sequences* $C(s,2)$ *for trace s from the previous example is equal to the set* $C(t,2)$ *for* $t = <a,b,c,d,c,a>$. *For* $k \geq 3$, *the call-sequence sets are different.*

To evaluate the usefulness of the model, we have used outgoing call-sequence sets to localize bugs. The idea of the approach is to use call-sequence sets extracted from passing runs to capture the normal behavior of objects. Differences in call-sequence sets from failing runs may then point to the cause of the bug. Our hypothesis was that the more a classes behavior deviates in the failing run, the more likely it is to contain the bug. In a controlled experiment with seeded bugs, our approach was able to localize bugs better than a comparable spectra-based approach.

The advantage of using a sliding window approach is a fine-grained control over the amount of temporal information contained in the model. Besides method calls, sequence sets could also be extracted from the same features as spectra. In this regard, the sliding approach is superior to the spectra approach. However, it is more difficult to relate sequences of features to locations in the source. In our work on bug localization [29], we had to resort to proposing all call locations in an abnormal sequence as potential bug locations.

To summarize, program spectra and call-sequence sets are fairly simple statistical execution models that mostly use control-flow information. Both approaches rely on counting to reduce the amount of data, thereby loosing parts or all temporal information from the execution trace. In the next section, we will present a class of approaches that use a more sophisticated formalism to represent dynamic program behavior.

3.4 Finite State Automata

A popular way to represent dynamic behavior is to learn a *finite state automaton* (FSA) from the execution trace. A finite state automaton is a directed graph with nodes representing different states of the system (i.e. the program state), and edges representing transitions between states. FSA permit having loops, that is (possibly endless) paths through the automaton that contain nodes several times. Loops provide a compact means to represent repetitive behavior. This makes FSA a good formalism for encoding program behavior, as execution information often is highly repetitive. In the remainder of this section, we investigate the problem of learning an FSA from a trace and present existing automata based software execution models.

3.4.1 Learning Finite State Automata

We start with the definition of a finite state automaton:

Definition 6 *A finite state automaton (FSA) is a 5-tuple $(Q, \Sigma, \delta, q_0, F)$ where Q is the set of states, Σ is the set of input symbols, δ is the transition function, q_0 is the start state and F is the set of accepting states. The transition function takes as input a state $q \in Q$ and an input symbol $\sigma \in \Sigma$ and outputs the (possibly empty) set of states reachable from q with σ.*

FSA are also well-known in language theory for their correspondence with the class of regular languages. Every FSA defines a regular language that is *accepted* by the automaton.

Definition 7 *We say that an FSA f accepts input sequence t iff the state q after processing t is in F.*

How can we transform an execution trace into an FSA? First, we formulate the *FSA learning problem* as follows: Given a set I of input traces, create an FSA that accepts all traces in I. Formulated this way, the FSA learning problem corresponds to the problem of learning a language based on a set of examples in the language. Fortunately, the problem of learning regular languages is well understood and has been thoroughly investigated. The seminal work on learnability by Mark Gold [48] proves that it is not possible to learn a regular language solely from a finite set of examples.

According to the proof by Gold, the main problem is that the learner does not know when it over-generalizes. To avoid over-generalization, the learner would require an *informant*, i.e. an oracle that can be queried if a given sequence is part of the language or not. However, in our scenario, there is no such informant and we therefore have to rely on positive examples only. As a consequence, it is not possible to learn a minimal automaton that only accepts all possible behaviors of a program solely from a set of traces.

For example, assume we have an alphabet $\Sigma = \{A, B, C, D\}$ and a trace $t = <A, B, B, C, D>$. Two automata that both accept t as input are depicted in Figure 3.4. The upper automaton accepts only t as input, whereas the lower automaton accepts all non-empty sequences of characters in Σ. While the first automaton is a precise representation of t, it will not recognize traces that are similar to t. Thus, this automaton is useless to find traces similar to t. On the other hand, the second automaton is too general, as it also accepts sequences that are totally unrelated to t. In practice, the level of precision depends on the application. Many applications are interested in finding an automaton that provides a compact representation of the input traces, but also permit slight deviations in order to identify similar behavior.

3.4.2 Software Process Models

Cook and Wolf [23] investigate the problem of discovering a software process model from a trace of *process events*. Events include any activity in the process, such as the creation of a document or the design of a component. As Cook and Wolf point out, such processes are often not stated explicitly, but rather manifest themselves in the trace of activities. A tool that makes the process explicit by

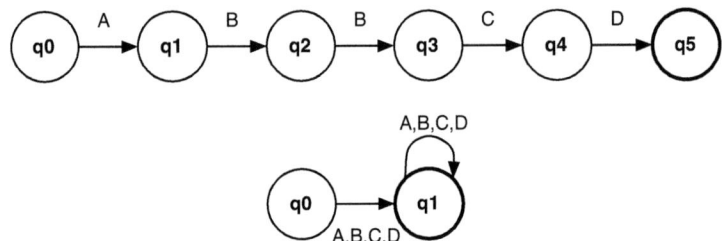

Figure 3.4: Two automata that accept input sequence "ABBCD". The upper automaton accepts only this sequence, whereas the lower automaton accepts all non-empty sequences that contain only letters A,B,C or D.

extracting a model from the activity trace allows to look for errors in the process and compare it to other process models.

Although software process models are slightly different from software execution models, the underlying learning problem is the same. Cook and Wolf were the first to investigate approaches that derive finite state automata from traces. In their work, the authors present three different methods for extracting automata, ranging from purely statistical to algorithmic approaches. We focus on the algorithmic approach, as it is also used by several other FSA based execution models[1, 70].

The *k-tail* approach devised by Cook and Wolf[3] assumes that a state is defined by the extent of different future behaviors that can occur. The future of a state s is defined as the k tokens that follow after a token in the trace. Parameter k controls the amount of temporal information maintained in the automaton. For larger values of k, the automaton contains more temporal information.

The k-tail algorithm is defined as follows[4]:

Definition 8 (K-Tail) *Let I be the set of sample strings, and let Σ be the alphabet of tokens that make up the strings in I. Let P be the set of all prefixes in I, including the full strings in I. Then $p \in P$ is a valid prefix for some subset of the strings in I, Let $p \times t$ be a string consisting of a prefix p and a tail t. Finally, let T_k be the set of all strings composed from Σ of length k or less. An equivalence class E is a set of prefixes such that*

$$\forall (p,p') \in E, \forall t \in T_k, p \times t \in P \leftrightarrow p' \times t \in P$$

Every prefix string is part of at least one equivalence class. Equivalence classes in E are mapped to states in the resulting automaton. For a given prefix p mapped to state E_i and a token $\sigma \in \Sigma$, the resulting automaton has a transition to all states to which the new prefix $p \times \sigma$ belongs.

An example of an automaton produced by the k-tail algorithm is depicted in Figure 3.5. Cook and Wolf made several improvements to the original algorithm that yield better results in the presence of

---
[3]This work is based on earlier work by Biermann and Feldmann [11]. We use the description given by Cook and Wolf.
[4]This description is taken from [23].

3.4. FINITE STATE AUTOMATA

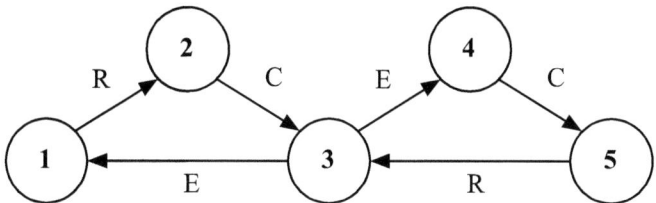

RCERCECRECRERCECRECRERCECRERCERCECRECR

Figure 3.5: Input sequence and automaton generated by the improved k-tail algorithm by Cook and Wolf [23] with k=2.

noise. In an evaluation, the authors found that the k-tail method generally produces good models in the sense that the inferred automaton reflects actual patterns of the process (e.g. sequencing, iteration), and there are no invalid states or transitions.

3.4.3 Extended Finite State Machines

Lorenzoli et al. [70] present an approach that extends finite state automata as presented in the previous section with information about parameter values. To that end, Lorenzoli et al. use DAIKON (see Section 3.5) to derive abstract predicates over parameter values of different method invocations. The resulting automata called *extended finite state machines* capture the interplay between parameters and temporal patterns.

An extended finite state machine is defined as follows (see [70]):

Definition 9 (Extended Finite State Machine (EFSM)) *For a given set of methods[5] M, a set of parameter identifiers U, and a set of global values V, an extended finite state machine is a tuple (S, T, s_0, s_F) where S is a set of anonymous states, T is the set of transitions, $s_0 \in S$ is the start state and $s_F \subset S$ is the set of accepting states. A transaction $t \in T$ is a tuple (s, s', m, P) where $s, s' \in S$ are the source and destination states of the transaction, $m \in M$ is the method that was invoked, and P is a set of predicates over the values of parameters and global variables associated with m.*

An example EFSM is depicted in Figure 3.6. As is obvious from the figure, the main difference to the approach by Cook and Wolf (Figure 3.5) is that transitions are labeled with method invocations and contain predicates over parameter values. In the example, predicates over parameters are separated from predicates over global variables by a horizontal line.

Lorenzoli et al. propose an extension to the k-tail algorithm called *gk-tail* that mines EFSM in three steps:

---
[5] In this thesis, we use the word method for both procedures and functions.

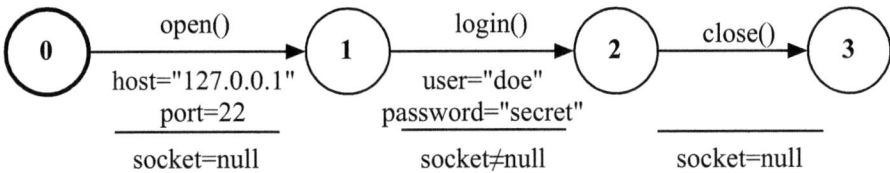

Figure 3.6: An example extended finite state machine. Predicates over parameters and global values are separated by a horizontal line (parameters above and global values below the line).

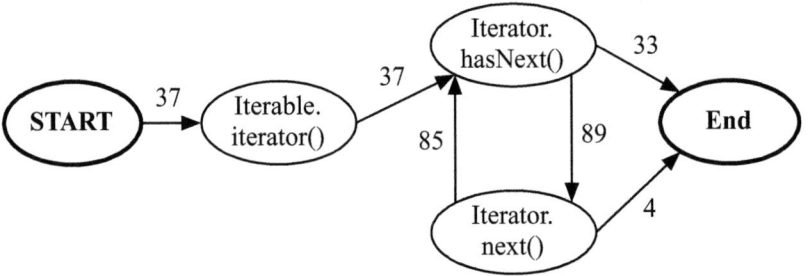

Figure 3.7: An object usage specification for the JAVA Iterator and Iterable classes. The edge labels denote the number of objects for which the usage specification contains the edge.

Merge Input Equivalent Traces In the first step, the algorithm combines traces with similar method call sequences. The intuition behind this step is that such traces often represent the same behavioral pattern.

Generate Predicates After that, the approach abstracts values of parameter and global variables into predicates using the invariant detection engine of DAIKON (see Section 3.5). In the example in Figure 3.6, DAIKON might infer that the port variable always has a value larger than zero. The derived predicates summarize the preconditions necessary to invoke the method.

Merge Equivalent States The final step uses the k-tail algorithm presented in the previous section to merge states based on the k future states. The precision of this step is again controlled by the value of k.

Lorenzoli et al. have used their algorithm to mine EFSMs for several open source projects. To evaluate the performance of their tool, Lorenzoli et al. investigated in how many cases the EFSMs were able to capture interactions that cannot be captured by finite state automata or invariants in isolation. The results of a preliminary evaluation with five open source projects show that EFSMs capture new properties for four out of five projects.

3.4.4 Object Usage Specifications

The approaches discussed in the previous section all use automata with anonymous states. States in these approaches carry no semantics that would allow to tell them apart. This lack of semantics is the reason why these approaches have to use sophisticated learning algorithms to deduce automata from execution traces. In this section, we present an automata-based approach that uses states labeled with the names of methods. The advantage of having identifiable states is that creating the automaton is significantly easier.

The approach by Pradel et al. [83] mines object usage specifications from an execution trace consisting solely of start and end of method events. In contrast to the approaches presented in the previous section, object usage specifications are specifically targeted at object-oriented languages. The approach is centered on the concept of object usage specifications, which describe legal ways to use one or more objects together. An example usage specification for the JAVA Iterator and Iterable classes is depicted in Figure 3.7. In the first step, the Iterator is created by invoking the Iterable's iterator() method. Afterwards, the iterator is traversed by alternating calls to hasNext() and next(). The transition labels indicate how often one method was invoked after another method. Transitions that end in state End indicate the last method that was invoked on the object before the garbage collector removed the object.

To mine such models, the approach needs to identify objects that collaborate. This is challenging, since execution traces typically contain thousands of object creations. To solve this problem, Pradel et al. only investigate possible collaborations for objects used within the same method invocation. The key assumption behind this idea is that methods implement coherent functionality, and therefore objects used within the same invocation are likely to be related. This idea greatly reduces the number of possible collaborations to investigate, and therefore makes the approach feasible in practice. Pradel et al. define an object collaboration as follows:

Definition 10 (Object collaboration) *Let a method call be a pair* (o,s) *of the receiver object o and the called method's signature*[6] *s. A collaboration is an ordered sequence*

$$S = <(o_1,s_1),\ldots,(o_n,s_n)>$$

of calls issued within the execution of a method (o_{outer}, s_{outer}). *Objects*

$$O = \{o \mid \exists (o,s) \in S\}$$

are said to collaborate.

Once the approach has identified possible collaborations, it proceeds by grouping related examples based on the set of methods in each collaboration. In this stage, the number of collaborations to investigate is still very high. Pradel et al. therefore discard collaborations with more than ten objects involved, and afterwards rank the remaining collaborations by the number of different code locations.

---

[6]In Java, a method signature encodes the parameter types of a method.

The intuition behind the ranking is that a pattern is more likely to be valid if it is used in different places across the program.

In the final step, each collaboration is transformed to a finite state automaton as follows: For each method s_i in the collaboration, a new state labeled s_i is added to the FSA. For each pair of consecutive method calls s_i, s_{i+1}, a transition from state s_i to state s_{i+1} is created, or, if the transition already exists, the transition counter is incremented.

In comparison to the approaches presented earlier, the step that creates the FSA is much simpler for two reasons: First, object usage specifications use labeled states, which makes state identification much easier. Second, Pradel et al. use only consecutive method calls for transitions which limits the degree of ordering information available with object usage specifications. If we provide the k-tail algorithm from Section 3.4.2 with the same input data, it would be able to detect more complex temporal relationships between method calls. In contrast to extended finite state machines (Section 3.4.3), object usage specifications only use control-flow information.

3.4.5 Markov Chains

Several automata-based approaches [15, 109, 56, 23] use *Markov chains* to augment automata with probabilistic information. In these models, transitions are labeled with the probability that a transition occurs. With this information it is possible to calculate the probability of a path through the automaton, or to cut off edges that have a very high or (depending on the application) a very low probability to occur. The theoretical basis of these calculations is the *Markov property*, named after the Russian mathematician Andrey Markov. Intuitively, a *Markov chain* is a sequence of states where all information about past states is contained in the present state:

Definition 11 (Markov Chain, Markov Property) *A sequence of random variables* $X_1, X_2, X_3 \ldots X_j$ *has the Markov property if* $\forall i \in \{1, \ldots, j\}$:

$$\psi(X_i = x | X_1 = x_1, X_2 = x_2, \ldots, X_{i-1} = x_{i-1}) = \psi(X_i = x | X_{i-1} = x_{i-1})$$

where ψ *is the probability that an event occurs.*

Markov chains can be visualized as directed graphs, with nodes representing different states of the system, and edges are labeled with transition properties. In the context of software execution models, states usually correspond to different memory states of the program.

Markov models are often used to model systems with unknown properties whenever it can be assumed that the unknown properties do not depend on historical information that is not part of the state description. A simple example of a Markov chain is the so-called random number line walk: The states of this system correspond to the entries on the number line (1, 2, 3 ...). At each state, the system advances to one of the neighboring numbers with equal probability. In this system, the transition probabilities depend only on the current state (the position on the number line) and not on the way the state was reached.

```
1  public static int gcd(int a, int b
      ) {
2    int r;
3    do {
4      r = a % b;
5      if (r > 0) {
6        a = b;
7        b = r;
8      }
9    } while (r > 0);
10   return b;
11 }
```

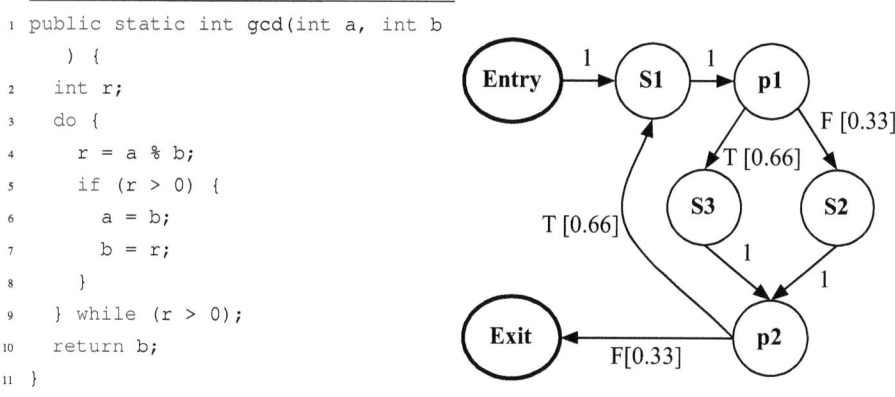

Figure 3.8: Example of a branch-based Markov model. Edge labels indicate the transition probabilities for each edge.

The advantage of using Markov chains is that the theory allows to calculate the statistical properties of the system given only the current state. Thanks to this property, Markov models are used in many different areas of research. One example of a software execution model that uses Markov models is the approach by Bowring and colleagues [15]. The goal of this approach is to automatically label program runs as passing or failing. To that end, Bowring and colleagues learn Markov models based on *branch profiles* of a program execution. A branch profile captures how often each branch evaluated true and false. The branch profile yields the probabilities for the transitions, while the structure of the model is derived from the control-flow graph. An example Markov model for the gcd method introduced earlier is depicted in Figure 3.8.

To distinguish runs as passing or failing, Bowring and colleagues train separate classifiers for a priori labeled training runs using a technique called *hierarchical clustering*. Clustering arranges similar models into clusters that represent the same behavior. To determine the distance between two models, the approach uses transition probabilities to cut off transitions below a certain threshold. Finally, models in the same cluster are merged by accumulating probabilities of shared edges.

The output of the machine learner is a classifier that can be used to label unknown runs as passing or failing. The labeling step exploits the Markov probability to calculate the probability of a new execution under each model in the classifier. If a model from the passing run yields the highest probability, the new execution will also be labeled as passing.

The authors evaluate the technique with a medium-sized application that contains real faults. They report precision values up to 0.97 for classifying over 13000 runs with a training set of up to 350 runs. Thus, the authors prove that the Markov property holds since the technique works very well. However, there is no proof that the Markov propert holds for the branch-based model.

3.4.6 Summary

To summarize, many software execution models use finite state automata as they offer a compact way to represent recurrent program behavior. They can be grouped into approaches with labeled states and approaches with unlabeled states. Learning automata with unlabeled states is equivalent to learning a regular language from a set of positive examples. Theoretical bounds prevent learning a minimal automaton that accepts a whole language, which is why learning models with unlabeled states is a trade-off between over-generalization and specificness. Some approaches interpret transition counts as probabilities and assume an underlying Markov model to calculate the probability of an event sequence given a certain model.

3.5 Invariants

The majority of software execution models use control-flow information only. However, control-flow is only a small part of the information available at runtime (see Section 3.1). Why is it that so many approaches do not take memory state into account? We believe that this is due to two reasons: First, there is a large number of variables that could be observed. Tracing all of them, as shown in Section 3.1 creates gigabytes of data, and is therefore infeasible in practice. Second, in contrast to variables related to control-flow (e.g. statement or instruction counters), the range of values for arbitrary variables is much larger. Also, there is usually no predefined semantics for individual values. Together, those two problems make it difficult to produce concise models based on the values of variables.

The first approach that tries to alleviate these problems is the DAIKON tool by Michael Ernst and colleagues [39]. DAIKON is a tool to automatically infer *dynamic program invariants* from executions. A program invariant is a property of one or more variables that is true for at least one *program point*. A program point is any point in time during the execution of a program. For example, one invariant might be that at the start of method foo, variable x always has a value larger than zero. Invariants may also express relationships between variables, such as the value of x always equals the value of y.

Internally, DAIKON traces the values of all interesting variables[7]. For each variable, the tool tries to match it against a predefined set of *invariant templates*. For example, one invariant template is that all values of a variable are larger than zero. A subset of all types of invariants supported by DAIKON can be found in table 3.2. This part, which is called the invariant deduction engine is by far the most complex part of DAIKON. It uses sophisticated techniques to reduce the number of invariants examined, and to find the most general invariant for each variable.

Together, the set of invariants DAIKON deduces from a program run form a software execution model based solely on the memory state at different points of the execution. DAIKON alleviates the problem of large variable value ranges by mapping values to a set of predefined invariant types. Combining different types of invariants and different variables allows for a flexible categorization which makes DAIKON a valuable tool for extracting properties of what should be achieved by executing

---

[7]The set of interesting variables is specified by the user. By default, Daikon includes all variables.

Invariant	Example	Description
OneOf	x one of $\{1,2\}$	This invariant indicates that a variable only takes a few distinct values.
LowerBound	$x \geq 0$	This invariant indicates that a variable does not fall below a certain lower bound.
Equality	$x == y$	Indicates that two variables always hold the same value. DAIKON computes sets of equal variables so that equality can also be detected for larger groups of variables.
NonZero	$x \neq 0$	A variable never takes the value zero.

Table 3.2: A subset of invariant types provided by DAIKON. In total, DAIKON supports over one hundred different invariants.

a program. However, in contrast to other software execution models, the set of invariants does not capture the temporal ordering of events. Thus, errors related to the sequencing of events can not be captured by this model.

3.6 Conclusions

In this chapter, we have provided an overview of existing software execution models. In an initial experiment, we saw that, even for short runs, observing all available dynamic information produces gigabytes of data. To be useful in practice, a software execution model needs to reduce the amount of data. This can be done either by restricting the model to a subset of all information (e.g. control-flow only), or by using abstraction.

Both program spectra and call-sequences use a simple counting approach to reduce the amount of data. As a consequence, these models do not contain information about the order of events, which is a vital part of dynamic behavior. A large group of approaches improves on this problem by using finite state automata to represent dynamic behavior. For automata with unlabeled states, it is necessary to use sophisticated learning algorithms in order to derive the automaton from an execution trace.

All of the aforementioned approaches put an emphasis on control-flow information, since there the range of values is limited. In contrast, the DAIKON tool uses a set of templates to deduce invariants that characterize the range of values for a variable. Such invariants provide a good abstraction over the values of different variables. However, a drawback of this approach is that invariants do not maintain the temporal ordering of events.

Overall, we found it difficult to provide a classification of software execution models. For most approaches, there is no theoretical foundation. Instead, many models are simply based on intuition. Most papers that introduce a new software execution model validate an approach by showing that the model yields good results for an application.

To summarize, the state of the art in software execution models is a set of approaches ranging from simple statistical representations to complex invariant mining. All approaches focus either on control-flow or on memory state, but there is no model that combines these two aspects of dynamic program behavior.

Chapter 4
Object Behavior Models

The previous chapter presented a survey of existing software execution models. In this chapter, we introduce a new type of software execution models. In contrast to most existing approaches that can be applied to arbitrary program languages, our approach is specifically targeted at *object-oriented programming languages*. In the object-oriented world, code and variables that are concerned with implementing an entity are grouped together in so-called *objects*. Objects communicate with each other by invoking *methods*.

We leverage concepts from the object-oriented paradigm to devise a new type of software execution models called *object behavior models*. An object behavior model describes the behavior of an object at runtime. Such models are finite state automata where states correspond to different states of the object, and transitions occur due to method invocations on the object. To characterize different states, we use the values of fields and the return values of so-called *inspector methods*. An inspector reveals information about an object's state to the outside world (see below).

Figure 4.1 shows an object behavior model for the JAVA Vector class[1]. The model consists of three different states:

"**start**" is the initial state of the object right after it was created (and before the constructor was invoked).

"**isEmpty():true**" represents an empty Vector, i.e. the list does not contain elements.

"**isEmpty():false**" correspondingly means that the Vector contains at least one element.

After adding an element to an initially empty list, the Vector is no longer empty. In the model, this is reflected by a transition from state isEmpty():true to state isEmpty():false labeled with add(). The remaining methods of Vector such as remove() or clear() change the Vector as we would expect from their names. Except for one transition, all methods invoked on the object terminate normally. The exception occurs if we invoke remove() on an empty Vector. In that case, the implementation of Vector raises an exception since it is not possible to remove an element from an empty list. In the model, this is represented by a self-loop in state isEmpty():true

---

[1] Vector is an array-based implementation of a list. It is part of the Java standard libraries.

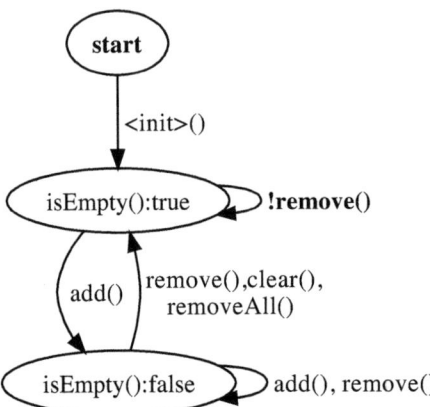

Figure 4.1: An object behavior model for the Vector class. The model relates method calls to changes in the state of the Vector.

labeled with !remove(). The bang (!) prefix is a convention used to mark method invocations that raised exceptions.

The object behavior model for Vector captures both the behavior and the usage of instances of Vector in a comprehensive way:

Temporal ordering The model maintains the temporal ordering of method invocations. For example, the first method that has to be invoked is the <init>() method, which is reflected as a single transition from start to isEmpty():true labeled with <init>().

Effects of method invocations The model captures the effects of a method invocation on the state of an object. For example, the first call to add() changes the value of isEmpty() from true to false. In addition, the model also shows that after a call to add(), the Vector is never empty. Such *post-conditions* represent important information that can be helpful in detecting bugs.

Exceptional behavior Finally, the model explicitly represents exceptional behavior as specially marked transitions (remove() in state isEmpty():true). This allows to distinguish normal and exceptional calls to the same method, and the different effects of such invocations.

Existing software execution models [23, 1, 83, 15, 109, 70, 56] also represent temporal information using finite state automata. However, this is the first approach that explicitly combines memory state and control-flow information. This is an important advantage, as it allows to relate method invocations to changes to an object's state. This information is vital for understanding how a class works.

Another advantage is that our approach does not need inference algorithms such as the k-tail method [11] to extract the automaton from the execution trace. Instead, we observe the values of fields and inspectors at the beginning and the end of each method invocation. Thus, we can transform the execution trace into a sequence of states and transitions (see Chapter 5). Deducing a finite state machine from this information is unambiguous and straight-forward.

In the example in Figure 4.1, the state of a `Vector` consists of the return value of `isEmpty()`. However, `Vector` also contains other inspector methods and fields. For example, one of these fields called `size` holds the number of entries present in the `Vector`. If we were to include `size` in the state representation, the resulting model would contain at least one state for each different size of the `Vector`. For a medium-sized `Vector` that holds up to 1000 elements, the resulting model consists of more than 1000 states. Clearly, such a model would not be helpful to understand how instances of `Vector` should be used.

For the example in Figure 4.1, we manually chose to only use `isEmpty()` to represent the state of a `Vector`. An alternative way that produces the same model is to use the `size` field, but only distinguish positive and negative values and zero. This way, we abstract the *concrete state* of `Vector` to an *abstract state*. This abstraction is what makes the model concise and meaningful. For `Vector`, our abstraction was influenced by a priori knowledge about the way `Vector`s work. However, if we want to extract object behavior models for classes with unknown behavior, such a priori knowledge is not available. To mine models for these classes, we need a general abstraction method that reduces the size of the models but retains important properties. Finding a good abstraction function is the most important problem we need to solve in order to fully automatically mine meaningful and concise object behavior models.

In the remainder of this chapter, we give a definition of object behavior models and discuss our approach for state abstraction. Xie et al. [113] concurrently developed a similar approach that also uses fields to characterize object states. However, their work does not investigate abstraction and hence the resulting models are very large.

4.1 Identifiers

We start with a definition of field and method identifiers. Since we initially developed our approach for JAVA, parts of the following definitions are JAVA specific. However, the underlying concepts are generic and it should be easy to adjust them to any other object-oriented language. We define method and field identifiers as follows:

Definition 12 (Method Identifier) *A method identifier m_{id} identifies a method. It is defined as a tuple $m_{id} = (c, n, s)$ where c is the fully qualified class name, n is the method name, and s is the method signature. c and n are defined according to the JAVA virtual machine specification [68].*

Definition 13 (Field Identifier) *A field identifier f_{id} identifies a field. It is defined as a tuple $f_{id} = (c, f)$ where c is the fully qualified class name, and f is the name of the field.*

Example 3 (Field and Method Identifier) *In the* `Vector` *example in Figure 4.1, the identifier for method* `isEmpty()` *is* `(java/util/Vector, isEmpty, ()Z)`[2]. *The identifier for field* `size` *is* `(java/util/Vector, size)`.

---
[2]Java encodes primitive boolean values using the letter "Z"

4.2 Inspectors

In JAVA, an instance of a class c consists of all accessible methods and fields defined in c or any of its super types[3]. Methods invoked on an instance of c usually operate on c's fields. Hence, these fields are an essential part of the object's state, which is why we also use them to represent an object's state in a behavior model. However, fields are not the only way to access an object's state. Many classes also provide state information to clients using so-called *inspector* methods.

Definition 14 (Inspector) *An inspector is a side-effect free method that takes no parameters and has a return value other than* `void`.

Example 4 (Inspector) *Method* `isEmpty()` *in the* `Vector` *example in Figure 4.1 is an inspector method.*

In a number of cases, inspectors simply return the values of fields[4]. If the field is also part of the state representation, including the inspector does not add new information. However, in some cases an inspector returns information that is not present in fields. For example, the `isEmpty()` method is an abstraction over the `size` field, namely that `size >= 0`. This abstraction is important for clients of `Vector`, and hence the developer decided to provide an inspector method for it. For object behavior models we can leverage inspectors to access such abstractions.

4.3 Value Access Paths

Now that we have decided which entities to include in the model, the next question is how to represent the value of a field or an inspector. For values of primitive type such as integers, doubles or booleans, we can resort to the string representations provided by the JAVA virtual machine. However, for object types (that is, fields that hold object references or methods that return objects) we have two different options: First, we could also use string representations as provided by the `toString()` methods. Unfortunately, as some classes do not provide unique object descriptions in `toString()`, this option cannot be used.

The second option would be to recursively include the state of referenced objects. Thus, a `Vector`'s state would also include the state of all objects stored within. In that case, including recursive state is not really helpful, as the state of objects in the list is not relevant for understanding how `Vector` works. However, if the contained object is an essential part of the containing object (for example if there is a part-of relationship between objects), including recursive state provides valuable information. Hence, we decided to provide the possibility to include recursive state in object behavior models. To be able to identify fields of recursively included objects, we introduced the concept of *value access paths*.

---

[3] In Java subclasses cannot access fields or methods that are declared `private`.
[4] Such methods are commonly referred to as *getter* methods.

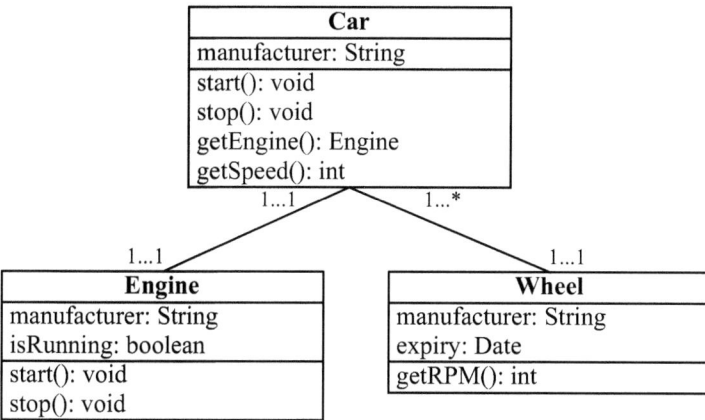

Figure 4.2: UML schema for a hypothetical car management application. A car consists of one engine and several wheels.

Definition 15 (Value access path (VAP)) *For a given set of field identifiers F and a set of method identifiers M, a value access path p of length n is a sequence*

$$p = <e_1, e_2, \ldots, e_n>, \forall j, 1 \leq j \leq n : e_j \in F \vee e_j \in M$$

of field and method identifiers that describes the path to obtain a value.

Example 5 (Value Access Path) *Figure 4.2 shows the UML diagram of a hypothetical application that models cars. If we recursively extract the state for an instance of* `Car`*, the value access path for the* `isRunning` *field of the engine retrieved via inspector* `getEngine()` *would be*

$$\langle (Car, getEngine, ()LEngine;), (Engine, isRunning) \rangle$$

A value access path allows for arbitrary combinations of inspectors and fields. It uniquely describes the steps to obtain the value at the end of the path. Value access paths are relative to an object and always start with a reference to `this`.[5]

4.4 Object States

A state in an object behavior model is a collection of value access paths together with the values. In the remainder of this chapter, we will use the letter D to refer to the set of values a field or inspector may take (in other words, the *domain* of a field or inspector). It consists of string representations for

---

[5]In Java, instance methods may access the associated object via the `this` reference. In other programming languages, `this` is also called `self` or `me`.

all possible values of primitive types in JAVA. An object state is a function that maps value access paths to values:

Definition 16 (Object State) *For a given set of field identifiers F and method identifiers M, an object state is a function $P \rightarrow D$ that maps value access paths in P to values in D.*

Example 6 (Object State) *For the* Vector *example, the object state after the constructor call is*

$$\{(\langle\langle java/util/Vector, isEmpty, ()Z\rangle\rangle, true)\}$$

Figure 4.3 shows a more complex example describing an instance of IMAPProtocol*, a class that implements communication with a mail server. Here, the object state right after the constructor call is*

$$\left\{ \begin{array}{l} (\langle\langle org/columba/ristretto/imap/IMAPProtocol, selectedMailbox\rangle\rangle, null), \\ (\langle\langle org/columba/ristretto/imap/IMAPProtocol, socket\rangle\rangle, null), \\ (\langle\langle org/columba/ristretto/imap/IMAPProtocol, state\rangle\rangle, NOT\_CONNECTED) \end{array} \right\}$$

It is possible to mix value access paths of different length in one object state. This is necessary since object references may be null, and thus we may be unable to extract all steps of a path.

4.5 Object Behavior Models

We are now ready to give a definition of object behavior models.

Definition 17 (Object Behavior Model) *For a given set of method identifiers M and field identifiers F, an object behavior model is a tuple (S, s_o, T) where S is a set of object states with value access paths of M and F, $s_0 \notin S$ is the starting state of the model, and T is the set of transitions. A transition is a tuple (s_s, s_t, I) where $s_s \in S \cup s_0$ is the source state, $s_t \in S$ is the target state, and $I \in \mathcal{P}(M)$ is the set of methods that label the transition.*

Example 7 (Object Behavior Model) *A textual representation of the model visualized in Figure 4.1 is available in Figure 4.4.*

4.6 Model Depth

As stated in the previous section, the state representation of an object o may also encompass fields of objects referenced by o. If state extraction is fully recursive, it may happen that the state of a single object encompasses large parts or even the whole state of the program. In most cases, such a model would be far too large to provide meaningful information.

To prevent such cases, we limit the depth to which recursive state is included and introduce a parameter called *model depth*.

4.6. MODEL DEPTH

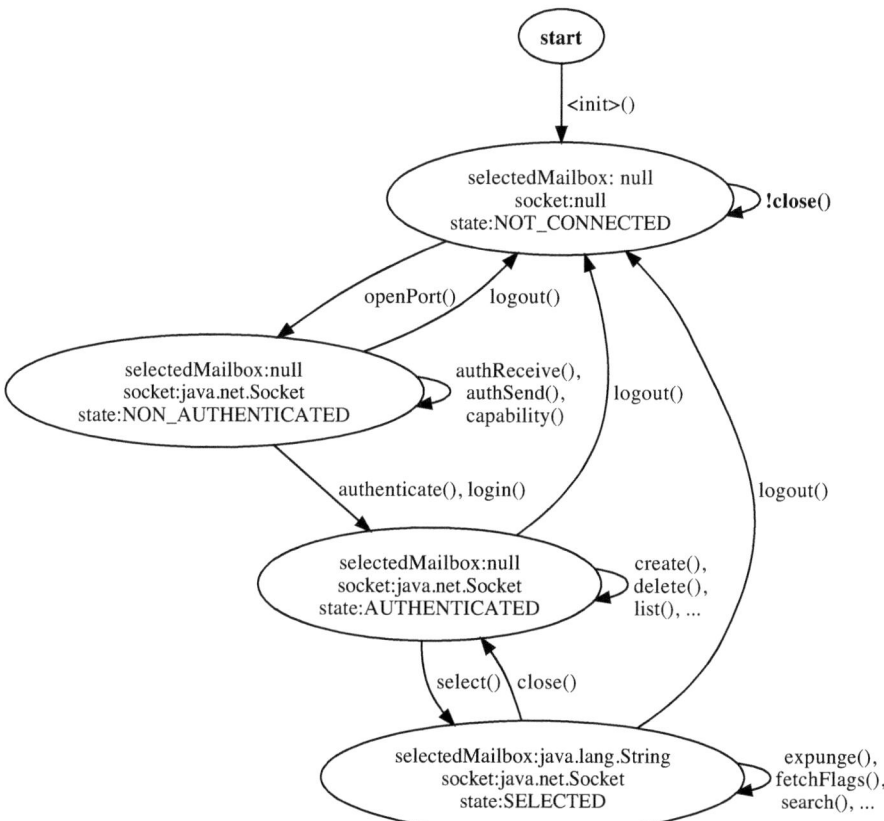

Figure 4.3: An object behavior model for the `IMAPProtocol` class. This class implements communication with an IMAP server and supports authentication and encryption.

$s_0 = start$

$S = \left\{ \begin{array}{l} (\langle(\text{java/util/Vector}, \text{isEmpty}, ()Z)\rangle, \text{false}), \\ (\langle(\text{java/util/Vector}, \text{isEmpty}, ()Z)\rangle, \text{true}) \end{array} \right\}$

$T = \left\{ \begin{array}{l} \left(\begin{array}{l} \text{start}, \\ (\langle(\text{java/util/Vector}, \text{isEmpty}, ()Z)\rangle, \text{true}), \\ \{(\text{java/util/Vector}, <\text{init}>, ()V)\} \end{array} \right), \\ \left(\begin{array}{l} (\langle(\text{java/util/Vector}, \text{isEmpty}, ()Z)\rangle, \text{true}), \\ (\langle(\text{java/util/Vector}, \text{isEmpty}, ()Z)\rangle, \text{false}) \\ \{(\text{java/util/Vector}, \text{add}, (\text{java/lang/Object};)V)\} \end{array} \right), \\ \left(\begin{array}{l} (\langle(\text{java/util/Vector}, \text{isEmpty}, ()Z)\rangle, \text{true}), \\ (\langle(\text{java/util/Vector}, \text{isEmpty}, ()Z)\rangle, \text{true}), \\ \{(\text{java/util/Vector}, !\text{remove}, (L\text{java/lang/Object};)Z)\} \end{array} \right), \\ \left(\begin{array}{l} (\langle(\text{java/util/Vector}, \text{isEmpty}, ()Z)\rangle, \text{false}), \\ (\langle(\text{java/util/Vector}, \text{isEmpty}, ()Z)\rangle, \text{false}) \\ \{(\text{java/util/Vector}, \text{add}, (L\text{java/lang/Object};)V), \\ (\text{java/util/Vector}, \text{remove}, (L\text{java/lang/Object};)Z)\} \end{array} \right), \\ \left(\begin{array}{l} (\langle(\text{java/util/Vector}, \text{isEmpty}, ()Z)\rangle, \text{false}), \\ (\langle(\text{java/util/Vector}, \text{isEmpty}, ()Z)\rangle, \text{true}) \\ \{(\text{java/util/Vector}, \text{remove}, (L\text{java/lang/Object};)Z), \\ (\text{java/util/Vector}, \text{removeAll}, ()V), \\ (\text{java/util/Vector}, \text{clear}, ()V)\} \end{array} \right) \end{array} \right\}$

Figure 4.4: A textual representation of the object behavior model visualized in Figure 4.1.

4.6. MODEL DEPTH

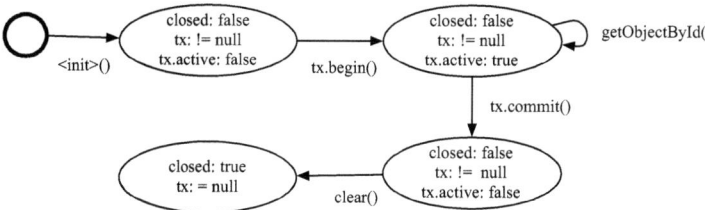

Figure 4.5: An object behavior model of depth two for class `PersistenceManager` of the APACHE JDO project. The manager uses a `Transaction` object to synchronize access to the database.

Definition 18 (Model Depth) *For an object behavior model m of object o, model depth depth(m) denotes the maximum length of value access paths in m. The minimum model depth of 1 includes only fields and inspector methods of o.*

Example 8 (Model Depth) *The examples in Figures 4.1 and 4.3 were extracted with model depth 1. Figure 4.5 shows a model of depth 2 for the* `PersistenceMan- ager` *class of the* APACHE *project (see below).*

By changing the model depth, we can adjust the level of detail in a model. For larger depths, the resulting models will contain more details. Which depth to choose strongly depends on the application and the examined class. We therefore use a default depth of one, but allow the user to specify a different depth value for each model.

One important aspect when mining a model for an object o is that for a depth larger than one, the set of methods used as transition labels may contain methods that are not part of o. This is best explained with an example: Figure 4.5 shows a model of depth two for the `PersistenceManager` class that belongs to the APACHE JDO project. This project is concerned with providing a framework to automatically store and load objects in relational databases. The `PersistenceManager` class is responsible for managing how objects are stored in the database. Internally, `Persistence- ¡Manager¿` holds a reference to a `Transaction` object that synchronizes access to the database.

For a model depth of two, the state of `PersistenceManager` also encompasses fields of its `Transaction` object. Whenever a method changes the state of the transaction, this change also affects the state of the `PersistenceManager`. In the example, the model contains a transition for method `tx.begin()`, which is invoked on the `Transaction` object.[6] Thus, the model captures the interplay between the `PersistenceManager` and the referenced `Transaction`, which is essentially a protocol that involves two objects of different types. The extent to which such protocols are captured depends on the model depth, which can be controlled by the user.

---

[6]To be able to relate such transitions to the fields that hold the reference, we annotate them with the value access path of the object on which the method was invoked (in this case, `tx` for the `Transaction` object).

4.7 State Abstraction

When extracting the state of an object, we store the values of fields or inspectors as strings[7]. Unfortunately, using *concrete values* for numerical values has a strong impact on the size of the generated models. For example, if a `Vector` model contains the concrete value of variable `size`, the resulting model will have a different state for each value of `size`. If the `Vector` grows to larger sizes, the model will become unmanageable and therefore useless. This problem gets even worse if a state contains several numerical variables.

To cope with this problem, we use a *state abstraction function* to map *concrete states* to *abstract states*.

Definition 19 (Abstraction Function) *An abstraction function* $f_{abs}: (P \to D) \to (P \to D')$ *abstracts the values of state* $(P \to D)$ *(cp. Definition 16) to a new state* $(P \to D')$. *Usually,* $|D'| \ll |D|$, *that is, the abstract state has a smaller range.*

To abstract a model, the abstraction function is applied to each state. As a result, some of the states are equivalent and will be merged, thus resulting in a smaller model. Obviously, this process entails a loss of information. A good abstraction function makes models small but retains all important information. Finding a good abstraction function is a problem in itself. Initial experiments with different functions showed that it is not possible to find a function that produces optimal models for all classes. Thus, our goal was to find a function that produces good performance for most classes.

Essentially, our problem boils down to finding a pattern behind a possibly large set of different values for a variable. Fortunately, there is already existing work that solves the very same problem. The DAIKON tool (explained in Section 3.5) by Ernst et al. [39] mines dynamic invariants from the execution of programs. Internally, DAIKON traces all different values of a variable and tries to find abstract properties using a set of predefined invariant templates. Invariants generated by DAIKON have been used in many different approaches[8] which gives rise to the belief that they can also be useful for object behavior models. Essentially, our abstraction function (called DAIKON-INIT) uses a subset of the invariant types implemented in DAIKON. Table 4.1 shows which types of invariants we use: Boolean values remain unchanged, numerical values are categorized as less than, equal to and larger than zero, and objects are either `null` or not.

In some cases this classification is too coarse: Many classes that are internally organized as finite state automata (typically, these are classes that implement protocols or streams) maintain state information using an integer field. These classes are of special interest as the corresponding models usually are a good characterization of the implementation. Unfortunately, DAIKON-INIT per se treats all numerical values the same and abstracts them as less than, equal to or larger than zero. We therefore developed a new abstraction function called DAIKON-ABS that improves DAIKON-INIT in two ways:

Limited value range fields If an integer field only gets assigned constant values, it is very likely that these values are important and thus the field should not be abstracted. To identify such

---

[7] For object references, we use a string representation of the object identifier (Section 5.1.5).
[8] For a summary, see http://groups.csail.mit.edu/pag/daikon/pubs/.

		Example	
Type	Values	Concrete	Abstract
Objects	$x = \text{null}, x \neq \text{null}$	`bar=#4711`	`bar≠null`
Numerical	$x < 0, x = 0, x > 0$	`foo=5.33`	`foo > 0`
Boolean	$x, \neg x$	`foobar=false`	`foobar=false`

Table 4.1: Abstractions used by DAIKON-INIT. Object references are either null or non-null, numerical values are less than, equal to, or larger than zero and boolean values remain unchanged.

fields, we run a conservative static analysis that identifies most of them. The list of fields is then passed to DAIKON-ABS which excludes them from abstraction. In the IMAPProtocol example (Figure 4.3), the state variable is a limited value range field and is therefore not abstracted.

Enumerations Since version 1.5, JAVA supports type safe enumerations. Internally, enumerations are implemented as an instance of the Enumeration class. In a sense, enumerations are object fields with a limited value range and therefore also should not be abstracted. Our static analysis recognizes enumerations and excludes them from abstraction.

4.8 Conclusions

In this chapter, we have presented a definition of object behavior models. Our models are finite state automata where states represent different states of an object and method invocations cause transitions between states. In contrast to existing software execution models, our models include both memory state and control-flow information. As a consequence, object behavior models express both the temporal ordering of events as well as the effects of executing methods. This makes our approach a versatile model for capturing runtime behavior of objects.

To be flexible, object behavior models allow using both values of fields and return values of inspectors to represent an object's state. Thus, we can derive models that provide different views of an object: A model based on inspectors soley uses information intentionally passed to clients in inspector methods. Thus, such models provide an external view of the object and its behavior. On the other hand, a model based on fields offers an internal view of the object. Different applications may prefer one type over the other.

In object-oriented designs it often is the case that one object forms an essential part of another object (part-of relationship). To be able to capture models of such objects, we allow to recursively include the state of referenced objects. The depth of the recursion is limited by the model depth parameter, which is specified by the user. This parameter allows to extract models on different levels of granularity, depending on the concrete application.

The crucial point about our models is the use of abstraction to reduce the number of states. An abstraction function is always a trade off between the size of the model and the information loss. The default abstraction uses the same categories of values as existing approaches [39, 67] augmented with information about constants and enumerations extracted from the source code.

Chapter 5

Mining Object Behavior Models

Mining object behavior models is a dynamic analysis that requires a lot of runtime information. As a consequence, collecting the required information and calculating the models is expensive both in terms of computation time and memory. We have implemented a tool called ADABU [1] that mines object behavior models from the execution of JAVA programs. We chose JAVA since it is a modern object-oriented language and because there is a broad range of open-source JAVA projects. This chapter describes important concepts that make mining models feasible in practice and also presents lessons learned along the way.

In essence, ADABU consists of two parts (see Figure 5.1): The *tracer* instruments the byte code of JAVA programs such that all information relevant for mining models is written to a trace file. The *model miner* processes the trace file to replay the execution and mine object behavior models. Separating model mining from tracing has several benefits: First, it allows to analyze a program run multiple times. This is especially important for multithreaded programs with non-deterministic behavior. Second, in order to mine models for languages other than JAVA, we only need to implement a new tracer for the target language and can reuse the model miner[2].

The following two sections describe the individual parts of ADABU. In Section 5.1, we present an overview of the tracer and explain several design decisions which provide valuable insights for other approaches that use similar techniques. In Section 5.2, we present the design of the model miner and highlight several aspects that are vital for the performance of the miner.

5.1 Tracing

5.1.1 Data Collection

The purpose of a tracer is to collect information about a program run in a trace file. The first step when implementing a tracer is therefore to find a way to collect the required information. In general, there are three different techniques that each have their own advantages and disadvantages:

---

[1] Adabu is the recursive acronym "ADABU Detects All Bad Usages." It is also the Swahili word for "good behavior".
[2] Chapter B in the appendix contains a detailed description of the trace file format.

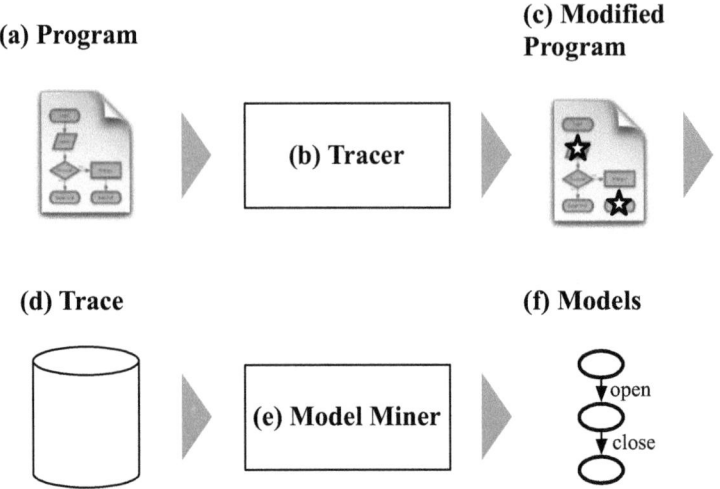

Figure 5.1: Overview of ADABU. The tracer (b) takes as input a program (a) and outputs a modified version (c). When executed, the modified version generates a trace file (d), which is fed into the model miner (e) to mine object behavior models (f).

Debugging Interfaces Programs written in languages such as JAVA or C# are executed within a virtual machine. Some virtual machines provide a debugging interface (e.g. the JVMTI interface for JAVA [58]) that can be used to access the state of the program. In principle, these interfaces can also be used to implement a tracer. However, there are two problems that make it difficult to apply this approach in practice. First, a new release of a virtual machine often also changes the debugging interface. As a consequence, a tracer implemented for the old version may not be compatible with the new interface. The second problem is specific to JAVA: Besides the standard implementation provided by SUN, there is a number of third-party virtual machine implementations. These implementations often do not support the debugging interface, and therefore the tracer cannot be used. Overall, relying on debugging interfaces limits the applicability of the tracer and is therefore problematic.

Source Code Instrumentation An alternative approach is to implement the tracer by adding additional statements to the source code of the program. The advantage of source code instrumentation is that it is independent of the target execution environment. Also, adding additional statements at the source level is only moderately complicated which facilitates implementing the tracer. The downside of this approach is that source code instrumentation, as the name suggests, requires access to the source code of the program. Since almost all projects make use of external libraries, it may be difficult if not infeasible to obtain the source code for all parts of a program. Hence, source code instrumentation is also difficult to apply in practice.

Binary Instrumentation The third option is to instrument binaries rather than source code. For languages such as JAVA or C#, this means to instrument intermediate representations (called byte code for JAVA or intermediate language for .NET). The main advantage of this approach is that it does not require the source code and is therefore easier to apply in practice. However, since intermediate languages are usually on a lower abstraction level than source code, binary instrumentation is more complex and thus error-prone than instrumenting source code.

Overall, binary instrumentation is the approach that has the fewest prerequisites in terms of the target platform and the required artifacts. We therefore chose this approach as the basis for our tracer. To cope with the increased complexity of instrumenting binaries, we have developed a number of best practices that will be presented in subsequent sections.

5.1.2 Architecture

There are several frameworks that allow to access and manipulate JAVA byte code. Most frameworks (e.g. BCEL [26], ASM [82]) provide direct access to byte code instructions. Other frameworks such as JAVASSIST [20] allow to specify modifications to the byte code using specialized languages. These modifications are then compiled and woven into the byte code. The advantage of having such a modification language is that the user does not need to deal with raw byte code. However, byte code weaving is complex and therefore these tools are rather fragile, which sometimes leads to incorrectly compiled code that is difficult to debug. Another problem is that the compiler generates many superfluous instructions, which often causes the modified code to exceed internal limits of the virtual machine such as the maximum number of instructions per method.

The aforementioned problems can be avoided by using a framework that provides direct access to the byte code. One such framework is ASM [82], which is used by many projects that analyze or manipulate byte code. ASM is designed according to the *visitor pattern* [45]. Inside ASM, visitors are organized as a chain (Figure 5.2) where each visitor processes the modifications generated by the previous visitor. This pattern allows to separate independent parts of the instrumentation into individual classes, which can easily be added or removed from the visitor chain. For example, if a user is not interested in tracing array access, the corresponding visitor is removed from the chain without affecting other parts of the instrumentation. The flexibility of this design is the main reason we chose to use ASM as the technical basis for our tracer.

The next step after choosing the instrumentation framework is to decide when to apply instrumentation. In JAVA, there are two options: *Pre execution instrumentation*, as the name suggests, instruments classes prior to the execution of the program. *On-the-fly instrumentation* uses the JAVA agent feature of the virtual machine to intercept all attempts to load classes and modifies the byte code before the class is being resolved. Both approaches are feasible solutions. However, on-the-fly instrumentation has the advantage that it allows to instrument all classes that are loaded. This is of importance for applications that generate new classes at runtime. To be able to analyze these applications, we have decided to implement ADABU using on-the-fly instrumentation based on the JAVA agent mechanism (Figure 5.2). Unfortunately, this entails other technical problems:

Preloaded Classes Classes such as `List` or `InputStream` are loaded before the JAVA agent is

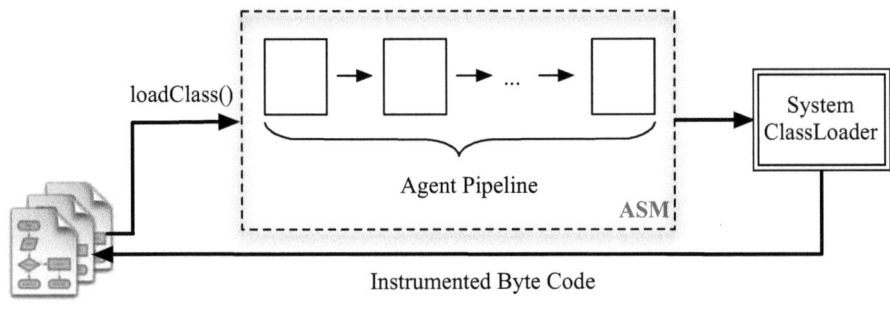

Figure 5.2: Architecture of the tracing framework. The tracer intercepts all requests to the class loader, transforms the original byte code with the agent pipeline and uses the system class loader to resolve the modified byte code.

activated. Hence, these classes will never be instrumented and cannot be observed. To cope with this problem, JAVA offers a feature to explicitly trigger re-transformation of already loaded classes. Unfortunately, re-transformation forbids to change the interface of a class or add new fields, which further complicates instrumentation (see below).

Multiple Instrumentation A considerable number of projects use their own strategies for class loading. Under certain circumstances it may happen that a class is loaded twice. In that case, instrumented code may be added more than once, which confuses the tracer and may result in incorrect byte code. To alleviate this problem, ADABU uses a *marker interface* to designate instrumented classes and only instruments classes that do not implement this interface.

5.1.3 Principles

Tracing information for model mining requires a fairly complex instrumentation. This complexity is mostly due to the variety of information (see Section 5.1.4) that needs to be collected. Instrumentation is further complicated by technical requirements such as independent treatment of different types of information and restrictions for re-transformed classes (see Section 5.1.2). These constraints, together with general problems when debugging instrumented byte code makes implementing a model mining tracer a challenge.

To cope with the complexity, the implementation of our tracer follows two important principles:

Minimize Injected Code The first principle is to use instrumentation only to collect data. More complex operations such as serialization and synchronization are handled in a special `Tracer` class, which is compiled JAVA code. As an example, Figure 5.3 shows byte code that writes data to a `double` field (bold instructions), and the instrumentation added by ADABU (plain instructions). The first six added instructions collect the target object of the field write and the

5.1. TRACING

ALOAD 1
DCONST_1
DUP2_X1
POP2
DUP_X2
DUP_X2
POP
DUP2_X1
LDC 0
ICONST_0
INVOKESTATIC java/lang/adabu/Tracer.fieldWritten
                                 (Ljava/lang/Object;DIZ)V
PUTFIELD TracingExample.foo : D

Figure 5.3: Byte code instructions added by ADABU to trace write access to a double field. Instructions for the original field write are printed in bold face. Code added by ADABU is printed with regular font face.

new value for the field. This data is then passed to the fieldWritten method of the Tracer class[3], which creates a FIELDWRITE event and serializes it in a thread-safe way. This way, the complex parts of tracing are handled by compiled JAVA code, which is much easier to debug.

No Local Variables Many tracing tasks require to temporally store data. In JAVA temporal information can either be put on the stack or stored in artificially created local variables. Using local variables for this purpose is much more complex, as the tracer needs to take care about the scope of these variables. Also, stack operations are faster than accessing local variables. For these reasons, the tracer avoids using local variables wherever possible and instead stores data on the stack. The downside of this approach is that it requires more byte code instructions to implement and sometimes complicates instrumentation. Figure 5.4 illustrates the effect of each instruction added to trace a field write for a value consisting of two words (Figure 5.3. Despite this slight increase in complexity, using the stack is the best way to temporally store data.

Together, these two principles reduce the complexity of the instrumentation and make the implementation more robust. We have successfully used ADABU to trace the execution of large programs with more than 50 000 lines of code.

5.1.4 Traced Data

The tracer produces one trace file per execution. This file consists of a stream of *events*, where each event captures an operation that is of interest to the tracer. Examples of events are the end of a method execution, instantiation of a new object, or read access to a field. The trace entry for every event

---
[3]Tracer is a singleton [45]. To avoid having multiple instances, the class must be part of package java.lang .

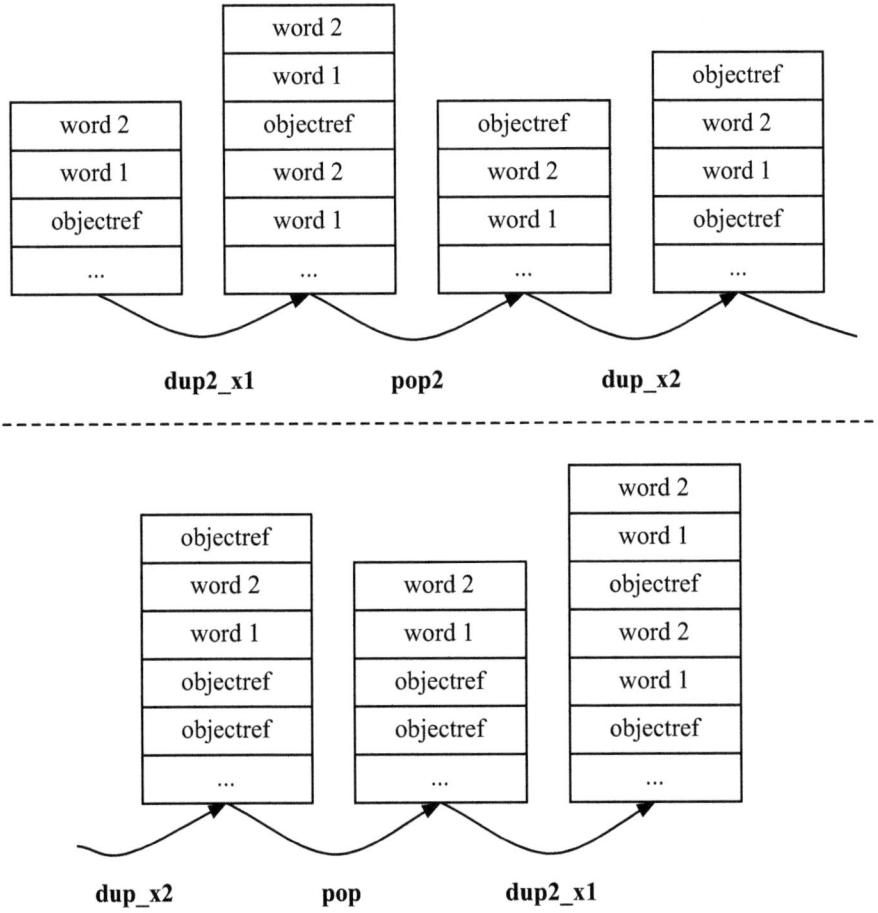

Figure 5.4: Duplicating the information of a field write operation (see Figure 5.3) requires a total of six byte code instructions. These instructions essentially duplicate the first three words on the stack.

contains all information associated with the event. For example, a method-end event specifies the name of the method that has ended, and the receiver object (for non-static methods). A complete specification of the trace format and the traced data is available in the appendix at page 145.

Most other dynamic analysis tools use a different approach to trace data. For example, the DAIKON tool [39] traces the values of variables and fields for every method invocation. Thus, even if a field is only changed once, a trace file generated by DAIKON stores the field value for every method invocation. In contrast, the event-based tracing approach of ADABU will only trace one event for the write access to the field. For extended executions, ADABU requires much less space to trace the same information as DAIKON.

5.1.5 Object Identifiers

Almost all events traced by ADABU specify a target object. For example, a field read event of a non-static field specifies the owner object of the field. Unfortunately, JAVA does not provide access to the identifiers used in the virtual machine and we therefore have to take care of object identification ourselves. As it turns out, obtaining unique object identifiers for JAVA is a difficult problem.

A first idea to approach the problem is to add an instantiation counter to each object. To implement this approach, we need to add a new field to every object, modify the constructor such that the identifier field is initialized, and provide a getter method for the instantiation counter. Unfortunately, re-transformation of classes (see Section 5.1.2) forbids to add fields, which is why this approach cannot be applied to all classes.

Another idea is to identify objects using hash codes as generated by the standard `hashCode()` method provided by `Object`. The default `hashCode()` implementation uses the address of the object in memory which would be sufficient for our purposes. Unfortunately, sub classes may override the default implementation and provide hash codes that are not unique throughout the program run. To solve this problem, ADABU uses the special method `System.identityHashCode(Object)` instead of the standard `hashCode()` methods. This method generates a unique hash code that ADABU uses to identify objects.

One catch with the above solution is that the generated hash code also uses the location in memory. Since the virtual machine may reuse addresses of deleted objects it is possible (though highly unlikely) that the same hash code is used for two different objects. To detect such collisions it is necessary to maintain a list of all garbage collected objects. However, since such collisions are rather unlikely, ADABU does not implement this feature right now.

5.1.6 Tracing Inspector Values

As explained in Section 4.2, the tracer should also trace values of inspectors as state information. To implement this, the tracer processes an XML file that specifies all inspector methods that are to be used. When instrumenting a class with at least one inspector, the tracer injects additional calls to all inspector methods at the beginning and the end of each method that is no inspector. The result of each call is then written to the trace file using the appropriate event code (see Section B.2.7 on page 152).

5.1.7 Multithreading

Since most modern programs make use of multithreading (for example, every JAVA program that uses a graphical user interface is automatically multithreaded), the tracer should also be able to handle multithreaded programs. This requires two changes in the tracer: First, information about reserved object identifiers (see Section 5.1.5) must be thread-local, since several constructors may be active concurrently. Second, each event needs to specify an identifier for the thread that triggered it. When analyzing the trace file, the model miner uses this information to group events triggered by the same thread.

5.1.8 Runtime Evaluation

Tracing induces a huge amount of runtime overhead, most of which is caused by I/O operations when writing the trace data to the disk. Table 5.1 presents the results of an experiment to quantify the runtime impact of the tracer. We have used ADABU to trace the execution of several subjects in the SPECJVM2008 benchmark suite, as well as the subjects in the IBUGS repository (see Chapter 6).

As explained in the previous chapter, ADABU supports specifying the set of classes to instrument. If the subject class is known before a run, a user can restrict tracing to this class, thus limiting the amount of tracing overhead. To measure the effect of limiting the set of traced classes, we ran ADABU with two different configurations: Tracing all classes and tracing only one class. For ASPECTJ and RHINO, we randomly chose ten different classes, ran the tracer for each class and recorded execution times and trace file sizes.

The results of our experiments are summarized in Table 5.1. Column *Runtime* lists the runtime of the unmodified program. Column *Overhead* gives the increase in execution time when running the instrumented program. Column *Trace File* lists the size of the generated trace file in gigabytes. Columns two and three specify overhead and trace file size for tracing all classes, whereas columns four and five list median values from tracing ten different randomly chosen classes[4].

When using ADABU to trace all classes, the slowdown is up to 400 times (`scimark.fft`). In general, the overhead for benchmark programs is much higher than for the two IBUGS subjects. This is at least partly due to the SPECJVM2008 programs being specifically chosen to measure the performance of a virtual machine. The IBUGS subjects on the other hand also perform I/O operations and are less intensive in terms of CPU usage. This difference in overhead indicates that, when used to trace interactive programs, ADABU incurs much less overhead than tracing CPU intensive programs.

When tracing only one class, ADABU incurs much less runtime overhead. For ASPECTJ, the slowdown is 30%, which is feasible in practice. If we know the set of interesting classes beforehand, we can configure ADABU such that the slowdown incurred by tracing is acceptable. However, if we are interested in models with a depth larger than one, it may be difficult to choose the set of interesting classes such that all relevant objects are traced. To alleviate this problem, we can use static program analysis to conservatively approximate the set of interesting classes and configure ADABU such that

---

[4]For the `crypto.rsa` benchmark there were less than ten classes. We traced all of them and also provide median values.

		Tracing all classes		Tracing one class	
Subject	Runtime (Seconds)	Overhead (Factor)	Trace File (Gigabytes)	Overhead (Factor)	Trace File (Gigabytes)
compress	3.2	320	75.2	170	40.3
crypto.rsa	3.6	178	35.8	23	2.2
scimark.fft	1.1	418	23.2	416	23.2
AspectJ	0.8	10	0.2	1.3	0.1
Rhino	1.1	5	0.0	2.3	<0.1

Table 5.1: Trace sizes and execution overhead for the compress, crypto, and scimark benchmark of SPECJVM2008 (upper part) and the subjects in IBUGS (lower half).

only those classes are traced.

5.2 Model Mining

After the tracer has finished recording the execution, the model miner processes the generated trace file to mine object behavior models. The input to the model miner consists of the following:

- The name of the trace file that is to be processed.

- A set of identifiers that denotes all objects for which the miner should generate models. Alternatively, the user can also specify a regular expression describing the class names of objects. In the remainder of this chapter, we refer to the set of objects for which models are mined as the *set of interesting objects*.

- An integer parameter that specifies the level of depth (see Section 4.6) at which models are mined.

Supplied with this input, the model miner processes the trace file to replay the program run, builds and maintains a representation of the program state, and mines behavior models by processing events associated with interesting objects.

5.2.1 Dynamic Heap Model

Most of the processing time in ADABU is spent on maintaining a *heap model* that represents the program state at runtime. In essence, the heap model consists of a set of *state objects*. Each state object represents one object that was created during the program run. The state object S_o for an object o is identified by the object identifier of o (see Section 5.1.5). It consists of a mapping of names to value representations. To identify fields, we use field identifiers as introduced in Section 4.1. Similarly, we use method identifiers to identify inspector methods (see Section 4.4). For values of primitive type,

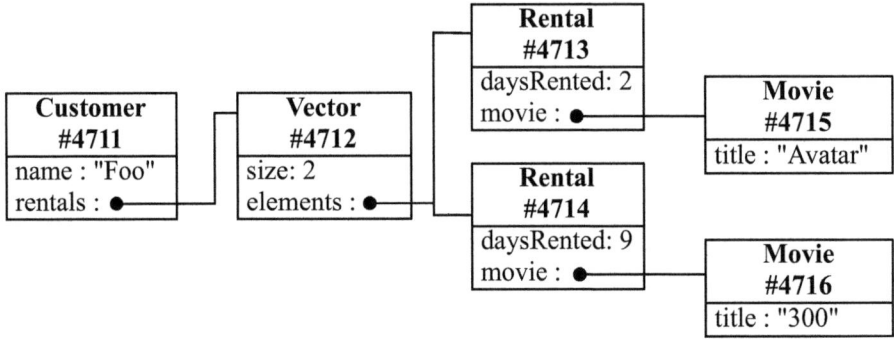

Figure 5.5: An example configuration of the dynamic heap. The `Customer` object uses a `Vector` to store references to `Rentals`, which in turn reference the rented `Movie`.

the mapping stores a string representation of the value. For non-primitive types (objects or arrays[5]), S_o stores the identifier for the object referenced by the field. To allow for fast access based on object identifiers, ADABU uses a hash map from object identifiers to the corresponding state objects. Figure 5.5 shows an example heap model based on the refactored design example in Fowler's book [42].

To build and maintain the heap model, ADABU processes the following trace events (see Table B.1 on page 154):

Object/Array Creation For each OBJECTCREATED or ARRAYCREATED event, ADABU creates a new state object with initially empty field information.

Update events Whenever a FIELDWRITE* or ARRAYWRITE* event is processed, ADABU updates the state of the corresponding object with the new value.

Naturally, maintaining a heap model of program runs with many objects requires a considerable amount of memory. One problem is that, in contrast to the virtual machine, the model miner does not know when it is allowed to delete states for objects. As a consequence, the heap model retains states for objects long after they were deleted in the run, which makes the memory problem even worse.

To improve on this problem, ADABU uses a simple analysis to identify objects that do not survive the life-time of a method invocation. The basic idea of the analysis is as follows: At the end of every method call m, ADABU deletes the states of objects that do not escape the execution of m. We did not analyze exactly how much memory is saved by this modification. However, with the modification turned on ADABU was able to process traces that could not be analyzed before.

---

[5]In the remainder of this section, we will omit discussion of arrays as they are treated almost identical to objects.

5.2.2 Model Generation

The implementation of model mining uses the dynamic heap model presented in the previous section. With an up-to-date dynamic heap model, implementing model mining is straightforward[6]. The most important tracing events processed are METHODSTART and METHODEND events. For every METHODSTART event, the model miner creates the following data-structures and pushes them on a thread-local stack:

FIELDSWRITTEN The set of fields written during the invocation. Each entry consists of an identifier for the field, the identifier for the object and the new value of the field.

OBJECTSCREATED The set of objects created during the invocation. An entry in this set consists of the identifier of the new object. This set is used to identify temporary objects as explained in the previous section.

OLDVALUES For fields that were changed during the invocation, this set stores the original values. Entries in this set have the same structure as the elements of FIELDSWRITTEN.

For every METHODEND event of a method *m* invoked on object *o*, ADABU pops the sets created at method start from the thread-local stack. If *o* is in the set of interesting objects, ADABU determines the set of changed objects *changed* that were altered by the invocation of *m* as follows:

- The set of changed objects *changed* is initialized to the set of object identifiers for which an entry exists in FIELDSWRITTEN.

- After that, ADABU removes all objects from *changed* whose value did not change. This is achieved by comparing the old value as store in OLDVALUES to the new value.

- In the next step, ADABU determines the set of objects *changed'* that reference objects in *changed*. It then merges all objects in *changed'* into *changed*. This step is executed *depth* times (see Section 4.6) to find all objects for which the changed fields may be part of a state in the model.

Example 9 (Changed Objects) *We use the heap state presented in Figure 5.5 as an example. Let us assume that the title of movie* #4715 *was changed from* Avatar *to* Avatar Directors Cut. *For a model depth of two, the set of changed objects is calculated as follows: In the first step, changed is initialized with object* #4715, *as this object was changed directly. The first iteration of the analysis adds object* #4713 *as it references* #4715. *The second iteration adds* Vector #4712 *for the same reason. In the next step, no new objects are added to the set and the iteration stops with*

$$changed = \{\#4715, \#4713, \#4712\}$$

---

[6]The presentation in this section omits the discussion of inspectors as they are treated the same way as fields.

Once the set of changed objects is calculated, ADABU updates the models for all interesting objects in *changed*. For a model n of object p that is currently in state s, ADABU first creates a new state s' that reflects all changes in `FIELDSWRITTEN` visible to p. It then adds a new transition from s to s' labeled with m to the model.

Model mining finishes as soon as the end of the trace file is reached. At this point, ADABU invokes a user specified abstraction function (Section 4.7) to generate the final models. In the end, the tool emits the mined models using standard formats such as DOT [5] or GRAPHML [16].

5.2.3 Runtime Optimizations

Maintaining the dynamic heap model requires ADABU to process large amounts of data. To make the tool scale to real-world programs, the model miner uses the following concepts:

Hashing ADABU makes extensive use of hash maps to be able to quickly determine information such as which objects are referenced by an object, and which objects refer to a particular object.

Integer Hashsets While implementing ADABU, it became obvious that the standard hash map implementation of JAVA uses too much memory. We therefore use an optimized version that uses primitive integers as keys, which significantly reduced the amount of memory used by ADABU.

Object Reuse Running a profiler on early versions of ADABU revealed that large parts of the computing time are spent on creating objects (for example, hash maps). To avoid this overhead, ADABU reuses objects to a large extent. Instead of creating new hash maps, ADABU maintains a pool of hash maps to which instances are returned when they are no longer needed. New instances of objects are created only if the pool runs empty.

Overall, our experiences with ADABU are positive. We have used the tool to mine models from the execution of large interactive programs. To allow other researchers to benefit from our work, we have made ADABU available for download (see Chapter 9).

5.3 Dynamic Side-Effect Analysis

As explained in Section 5.1.6, ADABU needs to inject additional method calls in order to mine models based on inspector values. A potential problem exists if the injected calls have *side effects*, i.e. they change the state such that the control flow and/or the output is altered. Models mined from such an execution are useless, as the side effects may affect the outcome of the run and hence the mined models may be incorrect. To be able to safely call an inspector method, we have to be sure that it is free of side effects.

Traditionally, methods that are free of side effects are referred to as *pure* methods, whereas methods with side effects are called *impure*. Classifying methods as pure and impure is called *purity analysis*. In some cases it is easy to establish whether a method is pure. In the example in Figure 5.6

5.3. DYNAMIC SIDE-EFFECT ANALYSIS

```
1  public void m(Object o) {
2    Vector v = n(new Vector());
3    v.add(2);
4  }
5
6  public Vector n(Vector v) {
7    v.add(1);
8    return new Vector();
9  }
```

Figure 5.6: Method n is impure because it modifies Vector v. Method m is pure because all modified objects are created during the invocation of m.

we immediately see that method n is impure because it modifies variables v and w. Method m however is pure, because it only modifies objects that are not visible externally. However, for complex methods manual analysis is tedious and error-prone.

Since manual classification is difficult, researchers have developed a number of automatic approaches to purity analysis. Most tools [76, 90, 101] use static program analysis techniques to identify pure methods. Unfortunately, these analyses do not scale well, which makes analysis of real-world programs difficult. The best static approach for JAVA by Sălcianu et al. [101] can only analyze projects that require JAVA 1.1, which prohibits analysis of most modern programs.

As static analysis does not handle the problem very well, we propose to use dynamic program analysis instead. In this section, we present a novel approach to purity analysis based on the observation of side-effects at runtime. Our implementation called JPURE uses ADABU to trace a program run, and analyzes the traces to classify all executed methods as pure or impure. If necessary, the classification can be further refined with data from other runs. To measure the degree of under approximation, we evaluate the precision of our dynamic analysis by comparing the results to the state-of-the-art static purity analysis. Our experiences when using output of JPURE with ADABU show that despite the under approximation, a dynamic purity analysis also produces reliable results.

The remainder of this section describes the definition of purity used by JPURE (Section 5.3.1), describes the algorithm used to identify pure methods (Sections 5.3.2, 5.3.3, and 5.3.4), and evaluates the soundness of our analysis (Sections 5.3.6 and 5.3.7).

5.3.1 Pure Methods

As a first step, we need to define when a method is pure. Previous approaches have used varying definitions of purity with different degrees of flexibility. For example, the analysis of Catano et al. [19] uses a definition that forbids a pure method to make any modifications to the heap. Many methods create and modify temporary objects that do not survive the execution of the method. Changes to these objects cause the analysis of Catano et al. to mark the method impure, although the changes never escape the method. Hence, this definition is too strict to be useful in practice.

For our approach, we define purity as follows:

Definition 20 *A method* m *is pure if it never modifies an object that existed prior to its invocation.*

This definition allows a pure method *m* to create and modify temporary objects and invoke impure methods as long as the side-effects of these invocations only alter objects created during the invocation of *m*. In the example in Figure 5.6, method *m* is classified as pure despite a call to method *n*, which is classified as impure.

5.3.2 Analysis

The idea behind our approach is as follows: For each invocation of a method *m*, we record identifiers of all objects created during that invocation. This information is used to calculate a *set of allocated objects* for each method invocation. In addition, we capture all field write operations and trace the identifier of the object that was changed by this operation (static field writes are recorded as changing a special object that represents all static variables). This information is used to calculate the *set of modified objects* for each method invocation. At the end of each invocation, we compare these two sets. Whenever the invocation of a method modifies an object which was not created during this execution, we know that the invocation changed externally visible state. Our analysis classifies a method *m* as pure if it was executed at least once and no execution of *m* modifies externally visible state. If at least one execution of *m* modifies externally visible state, *m* is classified as impure. The output of our analysis consists of a set of pure and a set of impure methods.

We have implemented our analysis for Java programs in a tool called JPURE. The tool works in two phases: In the first phase, one or more executions of the program to be analyzed is monitored (see Section 5.3.3) and trace data is written to a file. In the second phase (explained in Section 5.3.4) the trace files are analyzed and the tool classifies each executed method as pure or impure.

5.3.3 Tracing

JPURE relies on the tracing framework (Section 5.1) of ADABU to collect the required information. Due to its architecture, ADABU can easily be configured to trace only those events required by JPURE. The traced events include all method start, field write and object creation events (see Table B.1 on page 154).

5.3.4 Algorithm

Algorithm 1 summarizes the key parts of the analysis. For each method invocation we manage a set of objects created during the invocation (*newObjects*) and a set of objects modified during the invocation (*modifiedObjects*). At the end of each invocation we check for objects that were modified but not created during that invocation (lines 14–15). If at least one such object is found, the method is marked as impure. Otherwise, the method is marked as pure unless it was marked as impure in previous invocations. The last step at the end of each invocation (lines 20 and 21) propagates the sets of new and modified objects into the corresponding sets for the calling method.

For a given invocation of method *m*, Algorithm 1 computes method purity according to the criterion described in Section 5.3.1. Side-effects due to field writes in *m* itself are detected because

Algorithm 1 Compute purity information

Input: Trace File f
Output: List of impure and pure methods

```
 1: procedure PURITY(File f)
 2:     /* Initialize Datastructures */
 3:     for all event e ∈ f do
 4:         if e == METHOD_START then
 5:             newObjects.push(new Set());
 6:             modifiedObjects.push(new Set());
 7:         else if e == OBJECT_NEW then
 8:             newObjects.peek().add(objectId);
 9:         else if e == FIELD_WRITE then
10:             modifiedObjects.peek().add(objectId);
11:         else if e == METHOD_END then
12:             Set mObjects = modifiedObjects.pop();
13:             Set nObjects = newObjects.pop();
14:             Set escapes = mObjects.minus(nObjects);
15:             if escapes.isEmpty() then
16:                 /* mark method as pure unless it*/
17:                 /* was marked impure before*/
18:             else
19:                 /* mark method as impure */
20:             end if
21:             modifiedObjects.peek().addAll(mObjects);
22:             newObjects.peek().addAll(nObjects);
23:         end if
24:     end for
25:     emit results;
26: end procedure
```

we trace all field writes and instantiations of objects. Side-effects that occur in methods called by m are detected because the analysis propagates the sets of new and modified objects from all methods invoked by m. The algorithm also allows for m to call an impure method n (cf. Figure 5.6), as long as all externally visible side-effects of n modify only objects created during the invocation of m.

Our algorithm also handles field writes to transitively reachable objects correctly. For example, suppose that a method m changes field $o.x.f$ where o was not created by m (and thus the side-effect is externally visible), and x currently points to object l. If l was not created by m, l is not in the set of objects created by m and thus the algorithm correctly classifies m as impure. If l was created by m, there must have been a field write that set $o.x = l$ before. Our algorithm classifies this field write as externally visible side-effect since o was not created by m.

5.3.5 Multiple Program Runs

JPURE allows a user to provide more than one run as input to the purity analysis. We use this feature in the evaluation in Section 5.3.7 to analyze how much the soundness and completeness of our analysis benefits from additional data. If multiple runs are available, our tool analyzes them successively and updates the classification as follows:

- If a method m was not analyzed before, we add m to the set of classified methods.

- If m was analyzed before and the new classification is pure, the classification of m remains unchanged.

- If m was analyzed before and the new classification is impure, the classification is set to impure.

5.3.6 Soundness

Deciding whether or not a method has side-effects in general is undecidable. Thus, no analysis can be both *complete* (classifies all methods) and *sound* (all classifications are correct). Since our analysis is a dynamic technique, completeness depends on the amount of code covered by the execution. Purity analysis is a binary classification, so we distinguish two different types of soundness: An analysis is *p-sound* if all methods classified as pure are indeed pure. Conversely, an analysis is *i-sound* if all methods classified as impure are indeed impure. Our analysis is i-sound, because it classifies only those methods as impure that were experimentally shown to have side-effects. However, our technique is potentially not p-sound, since a method may contain code blocks with side-effects that are not executed. The evaluation in Section 5.3.7 measures the degree to which our analysis is not p-sound. The type of soundness required depends on the application that uses the results.

5.3.7 Evaluation

This section presents the evaluation of our tool JPURE. Our analysis uses the same purity definition as Sălcianu et al. [101], who have implemented their approach in a tool called PURITYKIT. We use the

5.3. DYNAMIC SIDE-EFFECT ANALYSIS

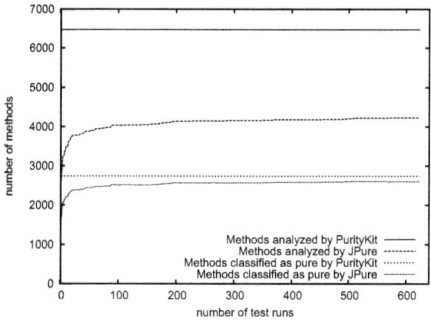

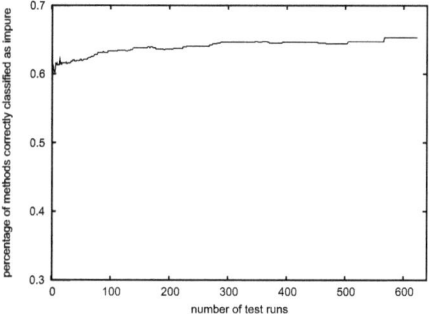

Figure 5.7: Purity results for ASPECTJ: Coverage increases from 29% at the beginning to 65% with all runs (upper graph). The percentage of methods correctly classified as pure increases as more runs are included (lower graph).

output of this tool as a ground truth for the purity analysis. Our experiments investigate the following questions:

Soundness How unsound is JPURE, i.e. how many entities are classified incorrectly?

Multiple Runs How do completeness and soundness improve if more than one run of a program is used?

Runtime Overhead and Analysis Time How big is the runtime overhead imposed by collecting trace information and how long does it take to process the trace files?

Measuring Soundness

To measure the soundness of the purity analysis, we calculate the precision values for correct classifications into pure and impure methods (similar to [3]):

$$\text{imp-prec} = \frac{ii}{ii+ip} \quad \text{pure-prec} = \frac{pp}{pp+pi}$$

ii is the number of methods correctly classified as impure, *ip* is the number of impure methods incorrectly classified as pure, *pp* is the number of methods correctly classified as pure and *pi* is the number of pure methods incorrectly classified as impure. imp-prec measures the percentage of methods correctly classified as impure, and pure-prec measures the percentage of methods correctly classified as pure. Ideally, both precision values should be 1.0.

For all experiments with the purity analysis, *pi* was always equal to zero and thus pure-prec $= 1$. This is because all entities classified as impure by our analysis were experimentally shown to be impure (cf. Section 5.3.1). On the other hand, our analysis misclassifies impure methods as pure if side-effects are statically possible but never occur at runtime. In the remainder of the discussion, we therefore only use imp-prec to measure soundness.

Evaluation Subjects

The following subjects were used in our experiments:

JOLDEN [13] is a suite of ten computationally intensive benchmarks which we included because Sălcianu also studies them [101] . We did not include the *power* benchmark in our evaluation since our tool ran out of memory when performing the analysis. *power* creates a large number of temporary objects and our tool tracks data for all of them, even after they are deleted, which eventually exhausts main memory. One way to improve on this would be to trace deletion of objects.

ASPECTJ [31] is a large program with approximately 75 kLOC which we used as the main subject to evaluate soundness and completeness of our tool. We study version #29934 of ASPECTJ as provided by the IBUGS [31] repository. We analyzed all 630 test runs available in the regression test suite that comes with the program. In order for PURITYKIT to be able to fully analyze ASPECTJ, we changed one line in the main class to directly instantiate a type rather than using reflection to do so.

ECLIPSE [38] is a large IDE for JAVA programs which we included to show how our tool performs on large interactive programs. We collected data from a run where we created a new class, typed in the body of a main method, compiled and executed the program and closed the workbench. Section 5.3.7 describes the runtime impact of our tool on the execution time.

The following sections discuss the results for the purity analysis and the runtime overhead of our method.

Results

We used the JOLDEN programs and ASPECTJ as subjects for our evaluation. The precision values for JOLDEN were slightly better than those for ASPECTJ, but coverage was much higher. We focus on ASPECTJ because it is a far more realistic subject than the JOLDEN programs. As mentioned in Section 5.3.5, our tool can analyze data from more than one run. We take advantage of this feature to perform a cumulative analysis of all tests in the test suite of ASPECTJ.

The results for the purity analysis are depicted in Figure 5.7. The upper graph compares the number of methods analyzed by PURITYKIT and JPURE. When run on ASPECTJ, PURITYKIT classifies a total of 6464 methods. The coverage values for JPURE range from 29% (one run) to 65% (all runs), meaning that JPURE classifies roughly two thirds of the methods classified by PURITYKIT. The precision evaluation uses only methods classified by both tools.

The lower graph in Figure 5.7 shows the effect of including more runs on the precision of the analysis. With data from one run, JPURE achieves a precision of 0.61. If all runs are included in the analysis, precision is 0.65, which means that our analysis incorrectly classifies 35% of the methods statically shown to be impure as pure. We investigated a sample of these methods. In many cases, the statements that are responsible for the side effects are either part of an if-else construct or belong to a method that is the possible target of a dynamically bound call. We also investigated how many times the classification of a method changes from pure to impure when adding data from another run. We found 171 methods where this was the case, which is a small number compared to the total number of classified methods (4231).

To summarize, 35% of the methods classified as impure by the static analysis show no side-effects at runtime. Using more than one run has a positive effect on the precision of our analysis, but the increase is not very strong (0.61 vs. 0.65).

Runtime Overhead and Analysis Time

Table 5.2 lists the results of our overhead evaluation. All experiments were conducted on an AMD64 machine with 2.1 Ghz and 2 GB of RAM. To capture the runtime overhead we divided execution times (as measured by the UNIX `time` tool) of a traced run by the execution time of an unmodified run. The resulting values are given in column *Overhead*. Column *Purity Analysis* lists the number of seconds it took to run the analysis. The values for ASPECTJ are mean values for all 630 runs of the test suite.

Runtime overhead for the JOLDEN benchmark (except for tsp) is generally much higher than for the other subjects (except for tsp). We attribute this to the fact that the benchmarks are purely memory-based and do not perform I/O-operations. The overhead for the non-benchmark programs ranges from 260 to 420%. Analysis times range from several seconds (treeadd) up to 20 minutes (bh).

To summarize, our tool induces a considerable amount of overhead for the purely memory-based benchmark programs, whereas the overhead for programs that perform I/O is acceptable.

Threats to Validity

Our evaluation only includes results for 10 programs, 9 of which are small benchmark programs. Therefore, we cannot claim that our results generalize to arbitrary programs. The main reason why we had to limit the scope of our study was that it is difficult to find subjects that can be analyzed by

Program	Overhead (factor)	Analysis Time (seconds)
bh	39.1	832.22
em3d	10.2	33.12
bisort	625.2	412.92
health	60.2	155.29
mst	28.8	602.12
perimeter	41.1	533.92
treeadd	8.1	389.72
tsp	3.2	158.53
voronoi	93.1	22.25
ASPECTJ	4.3	86.00
ECLIPSE	5.2	472.91
COLUMBA	3.6	182.17

Table 5.2: Runtime overhead and analysis time for JOLDEN benchmark programs (upper part) and interactive programs (lower part).

PURITYKIT.

Another threat to validity is the use of PURITYKIT as a ground truth. If the results of PURITYKIT were at least partly invalid, this would affect the correctness of our precision results. However, we manually verified a sample of the results and found no misclassifications. Besides that, [3] reports very high precision values for the mutability analysis of PURITYKIT, which gives us reason to believe that the purity analysis achieves similar precision.

5.3.8 Related Work

Side-effect analysis originated more than 30 years ago in the area of compiler construction, where it is used for optimization techniques. Early work by Banning [7] identified the problem of side-effect analysis. Cooper et al. [24] present a flow-insensitive side-effect analysis linear in the size of the call multigraph. These approaches were among the first to identify the core problems and the need for inter procedural analysis. Emerging techniques such as object-oriented languages further complicated the analysis. More recent techniques focus on the analysis of Java programs. Milanova et al. [76] use context sensitive points-to information to analyze each method invocation in the context of the object the method is invoked on.

Rountev [90] proposes a static side-effect analysis that can be parametrized by different types of class analysis. The paper compares results achieved with RTA to those for a context sensitive pointer analysis and finds roughly equivalent precision. Their purity criterion used is roughly equivalent to our criterion. However, the technique has difficulties with programs that use reflection, which holds for many modern programs such as ECLIPSE [38].

Xu et al. [116] describe a dynamic purity analysis. Their work explores several purity criteria ranging from strong to weak, whose definitions are strongly influenced by the proposed application, memoization. In contrast to their work, our analysis explores a well-established purity criterion. They also didn't evaluate the precision of their approach.

Sălcianu et al. [101] have implemented a static purity and parameter mutability analysis in a tool called PURITYKIT. The approach is based on a combined pointer and escape analysis and is the first to allow pure methods to modify objects created during an invocation. The main weakness of their tool is that it cannot analyze programs which require JDK 1.2 or above, while our tool has successfully analyzed modern programs with graphical user interfaces such as ECLIPSE [38].

5.4 Conclusions

We have presented key features of ADABU, a tool that mines object behavior models from JAVA programs. The tracing part of ADABU uses low-level code instrumentation to trace data for model mining because it is the easiest method to apply in practice. To cope with the complexity of a low-level target language, we divide the instrumentation into small parts that are organized as a chain of independent visitors. By limiting modifications to the stack wherever possible, we avoid hitting boundaries of the virtual machine. When tracing all classes of a program, the slowdown caused by tracing events for all classes is up to 400 times. If static analysis permits to limit the set of interesting classes, this overhead can be significantly reduced.

The model miner of ADABU builds and maintains a dynamic heap model that represents the program state. For every method invoked on an interesting object, the tool records the set of fields changed during the invocation. The heap model is then used to determine the set of objects for which the changes would be visible in the behavior model. If an interesting object is affected, the behavior model is updated with a new transition.

This chapter also introduced JPURE, a dynamic purity analysis that classifies a method as pure if it never modifies an object that existed prior to its invocation. The tool builds on the tracer of ADABU to collect the required information. To measure the precision of JPURE, we have analyzed 630 runs of ASPECTJ and compared the classification of JPURE to the output of PURITYKIT, a static purity analysis tool. In our experiments, 35% of the methods classified as impure by PURITYKIT never have side-effects, suggesting that there is a huge gap between static and dynamic purity. We have used the classification of JPURE as input to the ADABU model miner. Using this input, ADABU has successfully mined inspector based models from large interactive programs such as ECLIPSE and ASPECTJ. This shows that although the results of JPURE are unsound, the tool is still useful in practice.

In terms of lessons learned, the most important result from over three years of analyzing JAVA programs is that keeping the instrumentation part as simple as possible is vital to the success of any instrumentation-based dynamic analysis. In hindsight, using ASM as the basis of our work was a good choice. Its design enforces to split the whole instrumentation into several independent parts which facilitates implementation of the tracer.

Chapter 6
Mining Bug Benchmarks

The previous chapters presented the state of the art in software execution models and introduced object behavior models as a new type of models. In this chapter, we are interested in finding realistic subjects for the evaluation of our fix generation tool PACHIKA presented in Chapter 8.

In general, the scientific process to acquire new knowledge consists of two steps: First, a researcher devises a hypothesis. Second, this hypothesis is evaluated and the outcome is to either accept or reject the hypothesis. An evaluation can be made by proofing the hypothesis or by performing an experimental investigation. Since many problems related to bugs are undecidable in general, we will use experiments to validate hypotheses with different subjects and bugs. To avoid researcher bias, those subjects and bugs should not be developed by ourselves, but rather stem from external resources.

To yield reliable results, an evaluation should use realistic subjects and bugs. Unfortunately, existing repositories of bugs such as the Software-Artifact Infrastructure Repository (SIR) [37] provide mostly small subjects with artificially seeded bugs. An evaluation based on subjects from this repository would be flawed, because the results can hardly be generalized to realistic programs.

To avoid this problem, we have developed an approach to mine bug benchmarks from projects whose development history is recorded in a version archive. This chapter introduces our approach called IBUGS, presents existing subjects in the repository and analyzes the quality of the data. Parts of this chapter were published at the Automated Software Engineering Conference 2007 [31].

6.1 Motivation

A significant percentage of empirical studies focusing on testing concerns regression testing and are simulation studies. Many of them are based on (very) small programs and artificially seeded faults. [...] Furthermore, in most cases, the releases are not real software releases with real changes, and therefore, besides a handful of studies, it is unclear what kind of external validity can be expected from these results.

– Lionel Briand, Keynote ESEM 07 [17]

In the recent past, researchers have proposed a number of tools for automatic bug localization [117, 51, 66, 22, 67, 69, 121, 29]. Given a program and a description of the failure, a bug localization tool pinpoints a set of statements most likely to contain the bug that caused the failure. Although all approaches try to solve the same problem, many papers use different data sets to evaluate the accuracy of their approach. This makes it difficult for researchers to compare new approaches with existing techniques.

The Software-Artifact Infrastructure Repository (SIR) [37] aims at providing a set of subject programs with known bugs that can be used as benchmarks for bug detection tools. Subjects from the SIR have already been used in a number of evaluations [117, 51, 66, 22, 67, 69, 121, 29]. Despite the success of the repository, there are two issues with the current set of subjects. First, most of the programs are rather small and contain only few known bugs. Second, for the majority of subjects the set of bugs was artificially seeded into the code. In general it is unclear whether results for subjects in the SIR can be transferred to real projects with real bugs.

One reason why the SIR contains only few subjects with real bugs is that collecting such data manually is a tedious task. To alleviate this problem, we have developed a technique that automatically extracts benchmarks with real bugs from a project's history as available in software repositories and bug databases. The approach searches log messages of code changes for references to bugs in the bug database. For example, a log message "Fixed bug 45 298" indicates that the change contains a fix for bug 45 298. We provide faulty versions for bugs by extracting snapshots of the program right before the fix was committed. For each version we try to build the project and execute the test suite. Syntactical analysis of the fixes allows us to provide a categorization of bugs and to identify tests that are associated with bugs.

We have applied our approach to two projects: ASPECTJ is a compiler for an aspect-oriented extension of JAVA with more than 5 years of history. RHINO is a JAVASCRIPT interpreter used by MOZILLA. We assembled data from both projects in a repository called IBUGS and made it publicly available for other researchers.

Since our approach uses heuristics and relies on partially incomplete data such as comments, it may happen that we incorrectly classify changes or parts of changes as fixes. Such misclassifications may spoil the results of an evaluation based on the bugs in our repository. To evaluate the extent to which such misclassifciations occur, we use DELTA DEBUGGING [118] to minimize fixes for all bugs with executable test cases. Our evaluation shows that identifying fixes via commit messages causes a significant amount of noise.

In the remainder of this chapter we discuss related work (Section 6.2), explain our approach and practical experiences (Section 6.3), and present characteristics of subjects in the IBUGS repository (Section 6.4). Section 6.5 presents the results of our minimization experiment. Section 6.6 discusses results by other researchers that compared the ASPECTJ subject to other bug repositories in terms of possible bias. Section 6.7 ends the chapter with concluding remarks.

6.2 Related Work

We discuss the properties of existing benchmark suites, present a selection of bug localization approaches published in the recent past and what subjects were used for evaluation (see also Table 6.1), and summarize related work about bug categorization.

6.2.1 Existing Benchmark Suites

PEST. The National Institute of Standards and Technologies provides a small suite of programs for evaluating software testing tools and techniques (PEST). The current version contains two artificial C programs with each less than 20 seeded bugs. In contrast to the PEST suite, we aim at providing a set of real programs with bugs that actually occurred in the program.

BugBench. Lu et al. [71] describe a benchmark suite with 17 C programs ranging from 2000 up to one million lines of code. The paper describes 19 bugs the authors localized in those projects, with more than two thirds being memory related bugs that can never occur in modern languages like JAVA or C#. We could not further investigate the benchmark since we could not find a released version.

Software-Artifact Infrastructure Repository (SIR). The publicly available Subject Infrastructure Repository to date provides 6 JAVA and 13 C-programs, including the well-known Siemens test suite [89, 86]. Each program comes in several different versions together with a set of known bugs and a test suite. Subjects from the repository have already been used in a number of evaluations. A drawback of the current subjects in the repository is that the average project in the repository is only eleven kLOC in size while most real projects are much larger. Another problem is that almost all subjects only have artificially seeded bugs which often represent only a small portion of the bugs that occur in real projects. Using our technique to mine bugs from source code repositories, we can provide subjects for the SIR with a large number of realistic bugs.

Marmoset. The group around Bill Pugh collected bugs made by students during programming projects. Their MARMOSET project contains several hundred projects including test cases [97]. However, most student projects are small and not always representative for industrial development processes. In contrast to MARMOSET, our IBUGS project focuses on large open-source projects with industrial alike development processes.

6.2.2 Defect Localization Tools

Yang et al. [117] dynamically infer temporal properties (API rules) for method invocations from a set of training runs. The approach handles imperfect traces by allowing for a certain number of violations to a candidate rule. Violations of the rules in testing runs may point to bugs. Hangal et al. [51] try to automatically deduce likely invariants from a set of passing runs. Invariants are used to flag deviating behavior right before the program crashes in a failing run. Li and Zhou [66] mines programming rules from a program's code. Violations of these rules are flagged as possible bug locations. The previously described approaches provide an *ad hoc evaluation* with subjects that are sometimes not available to the public (like the Windows Kernel). Most of them also report only bugs they were able to detect, but

Approach	Language	Evaluation Type	Subjects
SOBER	C	Benchmark + Ad hoc	Siemens Test Suite, BC
AMPLE	Java	Benchmark + Ad hoc	JAVA Subject from Siemens Test Suite, four Bugs in ASPECTJ
Liblit05	C	Benchmark + Ad hoc	Siemens Test Suite
Cause Transitions	C	Benchmark	Siemens Test Suite
Predicate Switching	C	Benchmark	Siemens Test Suite
Perracotta	Java, C	Ad hoc	JBOSS Transaction Module, Windows Kernel
PR-Miner	C	Ad hoc	Large C projects (Linux Kernel)
Diduce	Java	Ad hoc	Java SSE, MailManage, Joeq

Table 6.1: Overview of evaluation methods for bug localization tools. Several evaluations use only ad hoc examples to evaluate their approach. Most papers that use a benchmark rely on subjects provided by the SIR repository [37].

omit information about bugs they missed. This makes it difficult for researchers to reproduce work by others and to assess the performance of their own approaches.

Several researcher improved on the lack of reproducibility by additionally testing their bug localization tools on publicly available benchmarks such as Gregg Rothermel's SIR. Cleve and Zeller [22] establish cause-effect chains for failures by applying DELTA DEBUGGING several times during a program run. Suspected bug locations are pin-pointed whenever the variable relevant for the failure changes. Liblit et al. [67] proposes a statistical approach that collects information about predicate evaluation from a large number of runs. Predicates that correlate with failure of the program are likely to be relevant for a bug. The SOBER tool by Liu et al. [69] calculates evaluation patterns for predicates from program executions. If a predicate has deviating evaluation patterns in passing and failing runs, it is considered bug relevant. Zhang et al. [121] automatically identify a (set of) predicate crucial for a failure. The suspected bug location is the dynamic slice of the crucial predicate(s). The AMPLE tool by Dallmeier et al. [29] captures the behavior of objects as call-sequence sets. Classes are ranked according to the degree of deviation between passing and failing runs.

6.2.3 Bug Classification

Several researchers investigated the phenomenon of bugs in the past. Ko and Myers proposed a methodology that describes the causes of software errors in terms of chains of cognitive breakdowns [62]. In their paper, they also summarized other studies that classify bugs. Defect classification has been also addressed by several other researchers: Williams and Hollingsworth manually inspected the bugs from the Apache web server and found that logic errors and missing checks for null pointers and return values were the most dominant bug categories [110, 111]. Xie and Engler demonstrated that many redundancies in source code are indicators for bugs [115]. Since such redundancies are easily caught by static analysis, this lead to an advent of static bug finding tools, such as FINDBUGS [54], JLINT [61], and PMD [55] (for a comparison we refer to Rutar et al. [91]). Typically, such tools take rules, and search for their violations. Recently, automatic bug classification techniques using natural language emerged: Anvik et al. used such techniques to assign bugs to developers [2] and Li et al. investigated whether bugs have changed nowadays [65].

6.3 Bug Extraction from History

Our goal is to exploit the history of a project to build a repository with realistic bugs that can be used to benchmark bug localization tools. We classify each bug by the characteristics of its fix, for example the size and the syntactical elements that were changed. For each bug we provide a compilable version with and without the bug as well as a means to run tests on the program.

The following steps are necessary to prepare a subject for the IBUGS repository. The sequence in which the steps are performed can vary, but some steps have to be performed before others (versions need to be extracted before they can be built):

1. Recognize fixes and bugs.
2. Extract versions from history.
3. Build and run tests.
4. Recognize tests associated with bugs.
5. Annotate bugs with meta information (size, syntactical properties).
6. Assemble IBUGS repository.

We first discuss the prerequisites for our approach and then present each step in detail. The number of bug candidates that we analyzed at the various stages are summarized in Table 6.2.

ASPECTJ: To illustrate how our approach works in practice, we describe our experiences with preparing the ASPECTJ compiler project as a subject. Paragraphs that are concerned with ASPECTJ are marked in a similar fashion as this paragraph.

6.3.1 Prerequisites

In order to be suitable for the IBUGS repository, a project needs to meet the following prerequisites:

	Number
Candidates	
– retrieved from CVS and BUGZILLA	489
– after removing false positives	485
– that change source code	418
– for which pre-fix and post-fix versions compile	406
– for which test suites compile	369
ASPECTJ dataset	
– bugs	369
– bugs with associated test cases	223

Table 6.2: Breakdown of the analyzed bug candidates for ASPECTJ. Many snapshots extracted from the version archive cannot be compiled.

Source repository (required). The project must provide access to a system like CVS or SVN where the project history is stored. We use the repository to identify changes that fix a bug.

Bug tracker (optional). The availability of a bug tracking system like Bugzilla or Jira helps eliminate false positives in the detection of changes that fix a bug.

Test infrastructure (optional). If the project has a test infrastructure we can use it to provide runs of the program. If there is no test suite available, the subject can still be used to evaluate static bug detection tools.

Our experience with open-source projects shows that all successful projects meet these requirements. Organizations like the APACHE and ECLIPSE foundations use a standard infrastructure with source repositories and bug trackers for all of their projects.

ASPECTJ: The project builds a compiler that extends the JAVA language with aspect-oriented features. It provides access to a CVS repository with over five years of history and a bug tracking system with more than 1000 entries. With over 75 000 lines of code excluding test code, it is among the larger open source projects.

6.3.2 Fix Identification

The first step in the IBUGS approach is to identify changes that correct bugs, in particular, bugs that were reported to bug databases such as Bugzilla. Typically, developers annotate every change with a message to describe the reason for that change. As sketched in Figure 6.1, we automatically search these messages for references to bug reports such as "Fixed 42 233" or "bug #23 444".[1] Basically every number is a potential reference to a bug report, however such references have a low trust at first. We increase the trust level when the message contains keywords such as "fixed" or "bug" or matches

---
[1] The format of references to bug reports is project specific. It depends especially on the bug tracking system that is used.

6.3. BUG EXTRACTION FROM HISTORY

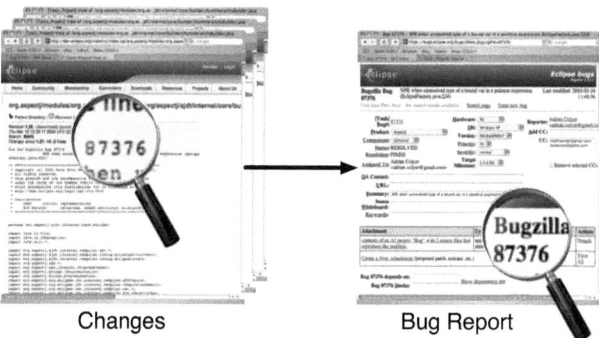

Changes → Bug Report

Figure 6.1: Bug reports are linked to changes in the version archives by analyzing commit messages. Keywords include bug identifiers and words like "Fix" or "bug".

patterns like "# and a number". Since changes may span across several files, we combine all changes made by the same author, with the same messages and the same time stamp (with a fuzziness of 200 seconds) into a *transaction* [125]. Finally, every change with a reference to a bug report is assumed to be a fix and serves as a candidate for our bug dataset. Our approach for mapping code changes to bug reports is described in detail by Śliwerski et al. [95] and is similar to the approaches used by Fischer et al. [41] and by Čubranić et al. [25].

ASPECTJ: We were able to identify 890 transactions that fixed a bug. We removed all bugs that took more than one change to be fixed, since we cannot be sure which change was really necessary to fix the bug. For similar reasons we did not consider changes that fix more than one bug. Altogether we found 489 bugs that were fixed only once in a transaction that fixed only one bug. A manual investigation of log messages revealed that four of them were actually false positives (the number in the log message accidentally matched a bug id) and had to be removed.

6.3.3 Extraction

For each bug we extract two versions of the program (see Figure 6.2): The *pre-fix* version represents the state of the program right before the bug was fixed, while the *post-fix* version also includes the fix. We then compare these two versions and remove all fixes that do not change the program code. This is necessary because some fixes do not affect the functionality of the program (like for example a misspelled dialog title in a resource file).

ASPECTJ: Altogether we found 67 bugs that did not change the source of the program and removed them from the IBUGS repository.

6.3.4 Test Execution

In the next step we prepare the pre- and post-fix versions of all bugs for execution (see also Figure 6.3). First we try to build each version. If the build process goes beyond a simple compile, most projects

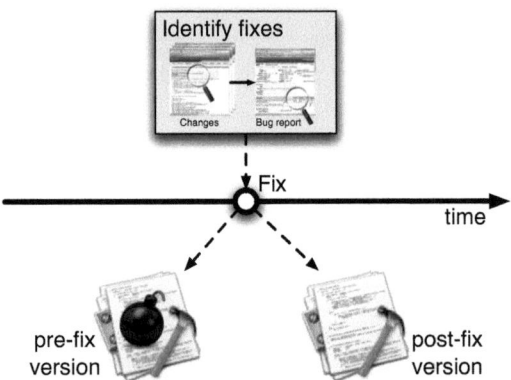

Figure 6.2: For each bug in the repository, we extract the pre-fix version right before the fix was committed. The post-fix version of a bug in addition contains the fix for the bug.

provide a build file. We identify the build file by examining the project and use it to run a build. Depending on the project, this may already include building and running a unit test suite. If this is not the case, we manually trigger the test suite and collect information about which tests were run and the outcome (pass or fail) of each test. After this step we remove all versions that fail to build.

ASPECTJ: The project provides a build file with separate targets for building and running the program and its test suite. We first tried to build the program and found twelve versions that had compiler errors. We removed those versions and tried to build the test suite for all remaining versions.

Building and running the test suite for all versions required a lot more effort than building the project. This is due to some inconsistencies in the test system and the fact that the test process changed several times over the history of the project. This caused (amongst others) the following problems:

- For some versions the tests cannot be built without having all modules in an Eclipse workspace.
- In some cases the program built fine but the tests had compiler errors.
- The names of build targets and output files changed several times.

We analyzed the changes in the test system over time to fix as many problems as possible. For 37 bugs we could not build the test suite and therefore removed them. The remaining 369 bugs were included in the IBUGS repository.

6.3.5 Associated Tests

Many dynamic bug localization tools [29, 22, 121] require a run that reproduces the failure and a passing run. While the project's test suite provides us with passing runs, it almost never contains failing runs for a previously unknown bug. This is because otherwise the bug would have been caught

6.3. BUG EXTRACTION FROM HISTORY

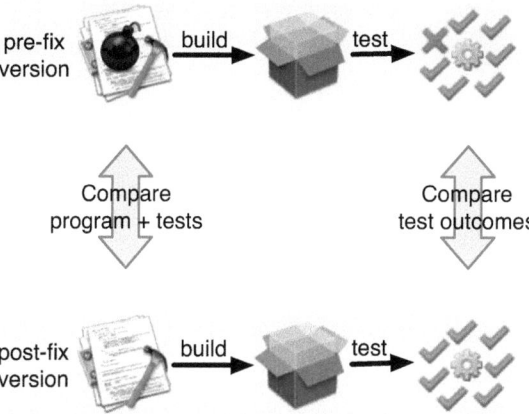

Figure 6.3: For each bug, we run the test suite on the pre-fix and post-fix versions and compare the output to identify failing tests.

already by running the test suite and we assume that developers run the tests before releasing the project.

To solve this problem we analyze the fixes for each bug and look for new tests that are committed together with a fix. The fact that a test is committed together with a fix is a strong indication that the test is related to the bug. Not all of these tests actually fail when executed since sometimes developers commit more than one test to check interesting cases that were discovered when fixing the bug. Bugs for which we can't find an associated test are not removed from the IBUGS repository, as they may still be useful for static bug localization tools.

The method to identify tests committed with fixes depends on the type of tests that are used in the project. However there is only a small number of testing frameworks used in practice and we can cover a lot of projects with techniques for the most popular ones.

ASPECTJ: The project uses two different types of tests. Unit tests are implemented using the JUNIT [44] framework, a popular testing framework for JAVA. Integration tests for the compiler (referred to as harness tests) are described in XML files. Our approach for identifying new JUNIT tests is straightforward: We examine all classes that were changed during the transaction that fixed the bug. A new test is found if a new subclass of `TestCase` was committed or a new test was added to an existing `TestCase`. New harness tests are found by analyzing the differences in the test description files. Altogether we found 223 bugs for which the fixing change added or touched at least one test case.

6.3.6 Meta Information

Some bugs may not meet the assumptions and prerequisites of a specific bug localization tool. For instance a tool may pinpoint to exactly one code location. In this case, bugs that span across several files would never be recognized completely by the tool and should be treated separately in the evaluation. In order to provide an efficient selection mechanism for bugs we annotate them with meta information about the size and syntactical properties of the fixes. When computing meta information, we ignore changes to test files and classes, since they are not part of the actual correction.

For each bug, we list the following *size properties* of the corresponding fix:

- *files-churned:* the number of program files changed
- *java-files-churned:* the number of JAVA files changed
- *classes-churned:* the number of classes changed
- *methods-churned:* the number of methods changed

For computing the size of a fix in terms of lines, we parse the so-called *hunks* returned by the GNU diff command. A hunk corresponds to a region changed between two versions. If the region is present in both versions, the hunk is called a *modification*, otherwise it is an *addition* (region is only present in the post-fix version) or *deletion* (region is only present in the pre-fix version). We use the line ranges of a region to compute the size of a hunk. Since for modification hunks the size may differ between pre-fix and post-fix region, we take the maximum in this case. In order to get the actual size of a fix, *lines-churned*, we aggregate the sizes of the hunks; we additionally break down the size to additions, deletions, and modifications.

- *hunks:* the number of hunks in a fix.
- *lines-added:* the total number of lines added.
- *lines-deleted:* the total number of lines deleted.
- *lines-modified:* the total number of lines modified.
- *lines-churned:* the total number of lines changed, i.e., the sum of *lines-added*, *lines-deleted*, and *lines-modified*.

From the bug report we extract *priority* and *severity* of a bug and include them as properties in our dataset. The priority of a bug describes it importance and ranges typically from P1 *(most important)* to P5 *(least important)*. In contrast the severity describes the impact and is one of the following: *blocker, critical, major, minor, trivial,* or *enhancement*. A severe bug may be have low priority when only few users are affected by a bug. However, in most cases bugs with high severity have also a high priority.

In addition to the above properties, we annotate bugs that produce exceptions with *tags*. We obtain this information by parsing the short description of a bug for keywords: *null pointer exceptions* typically are indicated by the keywords "NPE" or "Null", while *other exceptions* are indicated by "Exception".

In addition to size properties, we provide *syntactic properties* of changes. This supports the retrieval of bugs that were fixed in a certain way, say by changing a (single) method call or expression.

In order to express how a fix changed the program, we use the APFEL tool [122]. APFEL builds the abstract syntax trees of the pre-fix and post-fix version, flattens the trees into token sets and computes

6.3. BUG EXTRACTION FROM HISTORY

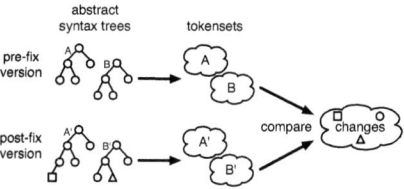

Figure 6.4: APFEL compares pre-fix and post-fix versions by converting the abstract syntax tree into a token set.

Token type	Description
Z–*expression*	Expressions that are used in casts, conditional statements, exception handling, loops, and variable declarations.
K–*keyword*	Keyword such as *for, if, else, new,* etc.
M–*method-name*	Method calls.
H–*exception-name*	Catch blocks for exceptions.
V–*variable-name*	Names of variables.
T–*variable-type*	Types of variables.
Y–*literal*	Literals such as numbers or strings
O–*operator-name*	Operators such as $+$, $-$, $\&\&$, etc.

Table 6.3: APFEL distinguishes eight different types of tokens.

the difference between these sets (see Figure 6.4).[2] APFEL supports different types of tokens for method calls, expressions, keywords, operators, exceptions handling, and variable usage. The type of the token is encoded in a single capital letter (see Table 6.3).

We use the differences computed by APFEL to create two fingerprints of a change at different levels of detail: The *concise fingerprint* summarizes the most essential syntactic changes such as method calls, expressions, keywords, and exception handling. In contrast the *full fingerprint* additionally records changes in variable names and contains more detailed information about the affected tokens.

- The *concise fingerprint* shows whether a bug (more precisely, its fix) is related to keywords (presence of the "K" character), method calls ("M"), exception handling ("H"), or expressions ("Z"). In contrast to the full fingerprint, the concise fingerprint omits variable usage, operators, and literals, i.e., it is a sub sequence of "KMHZ".

- The *full fingerprint* additionally shows variable usage ("V" and "T"), operators ("O"), and literals ("Y"). Furthermore, it specializes keywords (null, true, false, etc.), expression (if, while, for, cast, etc.) and operators ($+$, $-$, $\&\&$, etc.).

Figure 6.5 shows an example for a fix of a bug that caused a null pointer exception (NPE). The

---
[2]Note that APFEL is insensitive to the order of tokens because it relies on sets. This means that certain types of changes are missed such as swapping two lines.

```
1   TypeX onType = rp.onType;
2   if (onType == null) {
3  -    Member member = EclipseFactory.
4  -    makeResolvedMember(
5  -       declaration.binding);
6  -    onType = member.getDeclaringType();
7  +    if (declaration.binding != null) {
8  +       Member member = EclipseFactory.
9  +       makeResolvedMember(
10             declaration.binding);
11 +       onType=member.getDeclaringType();
12 +    } else {
13 +       return null;
14 +    }
15  }
16     ResolvedMember[] members = onType.
17        getDeclaredPointcuts(world);
```

Tokens changes computed by APFEL:

K-*else* (+1) K-*if* (+1)

K-*null* (+1) K-*return* (+1)

O-*!=* (+1)

T-*MethodDeclaration* (+1)

V-*declaration* (+1)

Z-if-*declaration.binding!=null* (+1)

Concise fingerprint:

KZ

Full fingerprint:

K-else K-if K-null K-return

O-!= T V Z-if

Figure 6.5: Fingerprints for Bug 87 376 "NPE when unresolved type of a bound var in a pointcut expression (EclipseFactory.java:224)".

differences computed by APFEL show that a new *if* statement was inserted: several keywords (*if*, *null*, *else*, and *return*) and the operator *!-* were added exactly once; APFEL additionally reports the new usage of the variable *declaration*, its type *MethodDeclaration*, and the condition of the *if*-statement. For the concise fingerprint, we omit the variable, literal, and operator tokens and the names of the other tokens. This results in the fingerprint *"KZ"*, telling us that keyword(s) and expression(s) were changed. In contrast, the full fingerprint contains all tokens, but omits names, except for keywords and operators. In the example of Figure 6.5 it is *"K-else K-if K-null K-return O-!= T V Z-if"*.

We included fingerprints in our dataset to support researchers when retrieving a set of bugs that match certain syntactic properties. Say, a researcher is interested in bugs that are related to null pointer checks. In order to come up with a set of initial candidates, she can query for bugs containing *"K-null"* in their fingerprint.

ASPECTJ: Fingerprints for all bugs in the IBUGS repository are provided in the description file *repository.xml*.

6.3.7 Repository

The IBUGS repository may contain several hundreds of versions for a program. For a typical project the size of a checkout from the source repository can contain 50 MB or more of data. This yields a size of several gigabytes for the IBUGS repository, which makes distribution difficult. We therefore create a new Subversion repository that stores the code for all versions. This greatly reduces the amount of space required to store the versions for the fixes included in the IBUGS repository. Meta information about the fixes in the IBUGS repository is stored in an XML file. For each bug we give information about the test suite, a pointer to the tests that were committed with the fix (if any), and the diffs for all files that were changed in the fix.

ASPECTJ: Snapshots of the project are approximately 60 MB in size. Although we have more

	ASPECTJ	RHINO
Size of code in latest revision (kLOC)	75	49
Number of commits to CVS repository	7947	2138
Number of tests in latest revision	1178	1248
Number of developers	13	17
Number of bugs in IBUGS repository	369	32
Number of bugs with associated tests	223	29
Size of repository (MB)	260	7
First bug report in IBUGS repository	2002-07-03	2001-05-03
Last bug report in IBUGS repository	2006-10-20	2003-12-07

Table 6.4: Statistics of the development history of ASPECTJ and RHINO. For ASPECTJ, IBUGS is able to link more bugs to transitions than for RHINO.

than 700 versions (two for each bug) in the IBUGS repository, the resulting file size is only 260 MB. Figure A.6 on page 143 shows an excerpt of the description file *repository.xml*.

6.4 Subjects

We have applied our approach to two different projects: ASPECTJ, a compiler for an aspect-oriented extension of JAVA, and RHINO, an interpreter for JAVASCRIPT written in JAVA. This section presents characteristics of both subjects and compares them in terms of the structure and the size of fixes.

6.4.1 Characteristics

The ASPECTJ compiler [59] consists of 75 kLOC and its test suite contains more than 1000 test cases. RHINO [78] is an interpreter for JAVASCRIPT that was incubated in 1999 by the MOZILLA foundation. With 49 kLOC, RHINO is the smaller of the two subjects. However, its test suite is a tad larger (1248 compared to 1178). Table 6.4 provides statistics about the development history of both projects.

Both ASPECTJ and RHINO are non-interactive programs that are controlled by the command-line. This makes it easy to write test cases, which accounts for the large number of tests in both projects. In general, the ASPECTJ developers put a stronger emphasis on meaningful commit messages. As a result, our approach links more bugs to changes in the source code, which is why the final number of bugs in ASPECTJ is much higher than for RHINO. For ASPECTJ, we identified 369 bug reports that changed program code. For 223 of these bugs, we also found associated test cases. RHINO has 32 bugs, out of which 29 offer an associated test case.

6.4.2 Locality

Figure 6.6 compares the locality of fixes for both projects. The histograms show the number of bugs that were fixed in one, two, three, four, five, or more than five Java files (left bars), classes (middle

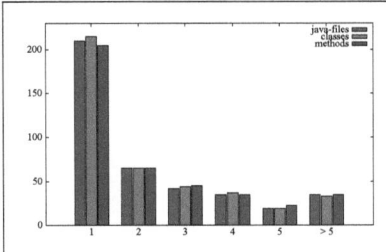 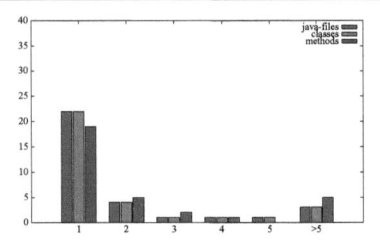

Figure 6.6: Histogram for touched files, classes and methods for fixes in ASPECTJ (top) and RHINO (bottom). The majority of fixes in both projects touches only one method.

bars), and methods (right bars), respectively. In both projects, the majority of bugs was corrected in exactly one method. This suggests that most bugs are local, spanning across only few methods. This is in line with our analysis of the ECLIPSE bug database presented in Chapter 2.

6.4.3 Size

Figure 6.7 shows the distribution of churned lines of code [3]. There are many small fixes for AsPECTJ: 44.4% of all fixes churned ten lines or less; almost ten percent of all fixes are one-line fixes, i.e., churned exactly one line. Only few fixes deleted code (about one third), most fixes modifies existing code (e.g., wrong expressions) or added new code (e.g., null pointer checks). Overall, the percentages of small fixes that we observed are consistent with the ones observed by Purushothaman and Perry [84].

For the bugs in RHINO, the fixes are generally larger: Only 20% of the bugs are fixed with changes to a most five lines, compared to almost 28% in ASPECTJ. The largest fix in RHINO touches over 2000 lines, compared to only 750 in ASPECTJ. One conclusion we could draw from these figures is that fixes in RHINO are more complex than fixes in ASPECTJ. However, it may also be that in RHINO changes classified as fixes are not minimal, i.e. they also include changes not necessary to fix the bug at hand. Section 6.5 examines this question in detail.

6.4.4 Syntactical Properties

In Table 6.5 we show the distribution of concise fingerprints for *small fixes* (i.e., five lines or less churned within one method) and *all fixes* of both data sets. The most dominant fingerprint is "KMZ" indicating that most fixes are of complex nature. Several fixes change only literals and variable names and therefore have an empty fingerprint. Exception handling (fingerprint with sub string "H") is exclusive to larger fixes, likely, because adding the skeleton of *try/catch* already takes four lines.

Simple fingerprints are most dominant for small fixes: Twelve fixes changed only method calls

---

[3] The number of churned lines is the number of added lines plus the number of deleted lines plus the number of changed lines.

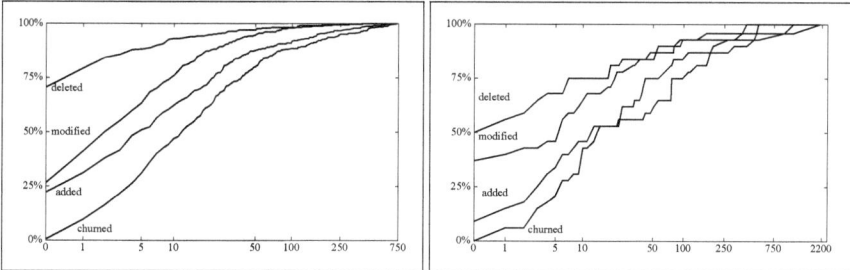

Figure 6.7: Cumulative distribution of deleted, modified, added and churned lines in ASPECTJ (top) and RHINO (bottom). Most fixes churn only few lines.

("M"), five fixes changed only keywords ("K"), and five fixes changed only expressions. The fingerprint "KZ" typically points to the addition of null pointer checks, that consist of a keyword (either *if* or *null* and an expression that checks for *null*).

We inspected all small fixes and observed mainly three categories: (1) fixes that change expressions, mostly checks for null pointers (presence of "Z" in the fingerprint), (2) fixes that add or change method calls (presence of "M" and absence of "Z"), and (3) other fixes (for instance empty fingerprint). For examples of fingerprints and characteristic fixes, we refer to Figure A.3 on page 140.

6.5 Minimizing Fixes with Delta Debugging

Due to the heuristic used to link changes to bug reports in IBUGS, it may happen that we incorrectly classify changes as part of a fix:

Misleading Log Messages When parsing log messages, we look for keywords such as "fixed" or "bug", as well as numerical identifiers that are used in the bug database. Since a comprehensive semantical analysis is not possible, we may classify a log message as describing a fix although this is not the case. One example of such a log message would be "This is a failed attempt to fix bug #4711".

Over sized Change Sets In theory, commits should be task-based, meaning that a single commit should only contain changes related to a single task. In practice, however, we encounter many commits that contain changes from several tasks. Thus, a commit correctly classified as fix may contain changes not required to fix the bug.

Incorrectly classified changes jeopardize the validity of IBUGS as a benchmark. If the repository contains too many irrelevant changes, the value of an evaluation based on IBUGS would be questionable. To provide a meaningful benchmark, we need to know what percentage of the changes in IBUGS are irrelevant.

One way to identify such irrelevant changes is to perform a manual investigation of the source code. This approach is problematic as it involves a lot of human effort and does not scale well.

	Fixes in ASPECTJ		Fixes in RHINO		
Fingerprint	Small	All	Small	All	Examples in Figure A.3
empty	6	33	1	2	Bug 132130
HK	0	2	0	0	
HKM	1	4	0	0	
HKMZ	0	32	0	3	
K	5	10	0	1	Bug 151182
KM	7	24	0	0	Bug 43194
KMZ	13	192	7	18	Bug 67774
KZ	20	31	1	3	Bug 123695
M	12	18	2	2	Bug 80916
MZ	10	16	1	2	Bug 42539
Z	5	7	1	1	Bug 69011, 161217
Total	79	369			

Table 6.5: Number of bugs per fingerprint in ASPECTJ and RHINO. Simple fingerprints are most dominant for small fixes.

Additionally, some bugs require expert knowledge of the system under study to decide if a change is really necessary. Thus, manual investigation is infeasible for a meaningful evaluation.

Our idea to approach this problem is to use a minimization algorithm called DELTA DEBUGGING [120]. To minimize fixes, we assume that a change that constitutes a fix can be split into several parts (for example lines or hunks). DELTA DEBUGGING uses repeated evaluations of the failing test case to identify relevant parts of the fix. To this end, the algorithm systematically applies subsets of the fix and tests each subset whether it is sufficient to fix the bug.

In the remainder of this section, we introduce the minimization problem and describe DELTA DEBUGGING (Section 6.5.1), and present the results of minimizing a subset of the bugs in ASPECTJ and RHINO (Section 6.5.2).

6.5.1 Delta Debugging

We suspect that for some bugs, not all changes of the committed fix are actually relevant to fix the failing test. Hence, we are interested in finding the *minimal set of changes* that are necessary to fix the failing test. This is an instance of the so-called *minimization problem*. To define the minimization problem, we first give basic definitions following the terminology introduced by Zeller et al. [120]:

Definition 21 (Circumstances, Outcome, Test Function) *Let C be the finite set of circumstances that are to be minimized. $\mathscr{P}(C)$ is the power-set of C that consists of all subsets of C. A test function $\mathscr{P}(C) \to \{✔, ✘, ?\}$ maps an element of the power set to one of the possible outcomes pass (✔),*

6.5. MINIMIZING FIXES WITH DELTA DEBUGGING

fail (✘) and unresolved (?). A set $F \in \mathcal{P}(C)$ for which a test function evaluates to ✘ is called a *failure-causing set of circumstances* with respect to the test function.

The minimization problem is then defined as finding the minimal set $F_{min} \in \mathcal{P}(C)$ such that test$(F_{min}) = $ ✘ and for all $G \in \mathcal{P}(C), |G| < |F_{min}| \rightarrow $ test$(G) \neq $ ✘. F_{min} is of interest since it denotes the minimal set of circumstances that together cause the test function to fail. Unfortunately, finding a minimal set of circumstances is a hard problem that requires to test all elements of $\mathcal{P}(C)$. Thus, an algorithm that computes a minimal set has exponential runtime[4], and is therefore not applicable to problems as they occur in practice (the largest fix investigated in our experiments touches 490 lines).

To circumvent this problem, Zeller and Hildebrand [120] propose to relax the minimization criterion to find *k-minimal subsets* instead of calculating a minimal subset. The *k-minimization problem* is to find a set T such that

$$T \subset C$$
$$\text{test}(T) = ✘$$
$$\forall T' \subset T, 1 \leq |T'| \leq k : \text{test}(T - T') \neq ✘$$

For a given k, k-minimality of a set T means that removing k or less elements from T will cause the outcome of the test function to change to ✔ or ?. However, there may exist $T'' \subset C$ with $|T''| > k$ such that test$(T - T'') = $ ✘.

Zeller and Hildebrand [120] propose an algorithm called DELTA DEBUGGING that calculates 1-minimal subsets with good average performance. The basic idea of the algorithm is that relevant circumstances are typically not distributed randomly, but rather form contiguous blocks. The algorithm exploits this fact by considering large contiguous blocks of circumstances in each iteration. DELTA DEBUGGING is best described by the following definition (taken from Zeller's paper [120]):

Definition 22 (DELTA DEBUGGING) *C denotes a set of circumstances for which the test function yields fail* test$(C) = $ ✘. *$P(C,k)$ denotes any partitioning of C into k equal parts. The* DELTA DEBUGGING *algorithm ddmin$(C) = $ ddmin$(C,2)$ is defined as*

$$ddmin(C,k) = \begin{cases} ddmin(C_j, 2) & \text{if test}(C_j) = ✘ \text{ for some } C_j \in P(C,k) \\ ddmin(C - C_j, max(k-1, 2)) & \text{if test}(C - C_j) = ✘ \text{ for some } C_j \in P(C,k) \\ ddmin(C, min(|C|, 2k)) & \text{if } k < |C| \\ C & \text{otherwise} \end{cases}$$

DELTA DEBUGGING works by continually partitioning the current set of circumstances and testing each set. For each partition C_j that fails the test function, DELTA DEBUGGING continues to

---
[4]For a proof see [80].

examine this subset (case 1). If no partition fails, it will consider the complement of each partition (case 2). Again, if no set fails the test function, DELTA DEBUGGING will increase the granularity for the partitioning (case 3). The algorithm terminates if no further elements can be removed from the set (case 4).

For a given set C and a test function, DELTA DEBUGGING computes a 1-minimal set of C [5]. The worst-case runtime is $O(n^2)$ where $n = |C|$. However, according to Neuhaus [80], DELTA DEBUGGING executes much faster in practice. It has been successfully applied in different areas of computer science including software engineering [120, 22, 100] and security [81].

6.5.2 Minimizing Fixes

In the context of minimizing fixes, we define the set of circumstances and the test function as follows:

Circumstances Every bug is fixed by a single commit to the version archive. To minimize the commit, it is necessary to further split it into a set of changes that each add, remove, or change *a single line*. This set of changes forms the set of circumstances for minimizing fixes.

Test Function The test function evaluates whether a given subset of changes is a fix for the bug at hand. To automate the test function, we rely on the existence of a regression test suite that contains at least one failing test to reproduce the problem, and one or more passing tests. To fix a bug, a set of changes C_{fix} has to meet the following conditions:

1. Applying C_{fix} alters the outcome of the failing test from fail to pass.
2. Applying C_{fix} does not change the outcome of any of the passing tests.

The first condition tests that C_{fix} actually fixes the problem, whereas the second condition ensures that the fix does not break any other tests in the test suite.

Experimental Setup

To perform the experiments, we use a publicly available implementation of DELTA DEBUGGING called DDCHANGE [18]. We use all bugs of ASPECTJ and RHINO that provide an associated test case that fails in the pre-fix version and passes in the post-fix version. This is to ensure that the test case is actually related to the bug, and the change applied actually fixes the problem. Altogether we found 15 bugs in RHINO, and 33 bugs in ASPECTJ.

In order to minimize a problem, DDCHANGE requires a test function that evaluates a set of changes. In our setting, the test function (1) applies the set of changes, (2) tries to compile the modified program, and (3) executes the test suite to determine the test outcome. Depending on the results of steps 2 and 3, the test function produces the following result:

Unresolved (?) The modified program cannot be compiled.

---
[5] A proof is available in [120].

6.5. MINIMIZING FIXES WITH DELTA DEBUGGING 81

Fail (✘) The program compiles and all tests (including the failing test) pass. This is somewhat counter-intuitive, as DELTA DEBUGGING was initially designed to minimize failure inducing input and therefore is interested in sets of changes that cause the test to fail. However, in our setting we look for changes that cause the failing test to pass and hence swap the meaning of pass and fail.

Pass (✔) The program compiles but at least one test in the test suite fails.

As explained above, including the whole test suite is important to make sure that the minimized set of changes not only fixes the bug, but also does not break other aspects of the program. To study the importance of considering all tests in the test function, we repeat our experiments twice: In the first run, we consider only the failing test, whereas in the second run we also include the remaining tests of the test suite.

Results

The results of our experiments with RHINO are summarized in Table 6.6. Tables 6.7 and 6.8 show results for ASPECTJ. Column *Bug Id* lists the bug identifier for each bug included in the study. Column *Size of Fix* gives the size of each fix in terms of the number of churned[6] lines. Since some fixes also change comments, we also give the fraction of non-comment lines churned in column three. Columns four and five list the minimization results in terms of the fraction of relevant lines when only considering the failing run (column four) and for the whole test suite (column five).

To aggregate the results, we provide average ($\emptyset$) and median (~) values in the last two rows of each table. Since average values can be misleading if the data is not normally distributed, we first check whether the data is normally distributed. To that end, we compare each row against a normal distribution using a Kolmogorov-Smirnov test [14]. Parameters for the normal distribution are estimated using the maximum likelihood method. The results of the Kolmogorov-Smirnov test reveal that the data is not normally distributed, which tells us that the average values should not be used. In the remainder of this section we will therefore only use median values when interpreting data.

Based on the values in Tables 6.6 and 6.7 we make the following observations:

Size of Fixes The median size of a fix is roughly equivalent for both projects (11 lines for ASPECTJ compared to 14 lines for RHINO). Considering the size distribution of all bugs presented in Figure 6.7, we can conclude that bugs included in our evaluation are slightly larger than the normal bug in the repository. An interesting observation is the big gap between average and median sizes. For RHINO, a few bugs with very large fixes are enough to tilt the average towards a misleadingly high number. This highlights the importance of using median values to analyze the data.

Comments In terms of comments, we observe that fixes for RHINO typically contain much fewer comments than fixes for ASPECTJ. As comments are important for the maintenance of a project,

---
[6]Churned lines consists of added, deleted and changed lines.

	Size of Fix (Lines)	Fraction of Non-Comment Lines	Minimization Results	
Bug Id			Failing Test Only	All Tests
#114491	10	1.00	0.90	0.90
#114493	3	1.00	0.33	0.33
#137181	66	0.94	0.64	0.86
#157509	310	0.90	0.05	0.63
#159334	58	1.00	0.31	0.36
#177314	10	0.90	0.20	0.50
#179068	173	0.91	0.03	0.50
#181654	23	0.96	0.78	0.96
#181834	14	0.93	0.07	0.36
#193555	115	0.97	0.01	0.01
#194364	5	1.00	0.60	0.80
#203402	3	1.00	0.33	1.00
#203841	490	0.97	0.52	0.65
#210682	8	1.00	0.75	0.75
#220584	4	1.00	1.00	1.00
∅	**88**	**0.96**	**0.43**	**0.64**
~	**14**	**0.97**	**0.33**	**0.65**

Table 6.6: Minimization results for RHINO. For example, the fix for bug #177314 touches 10 lines, out of which 1 is a comment. Minimizing with the failing run only removes 7 more lines, whereas when considering the whole test suite, only 4 lines can be removed. Overall, if minimization uses only the failing test, DELTA DEBUGGING considers the majority of lines irrelevant for fixing the bug.

	Size of Fix	Fraction of Non-	Minimization Results	
			Failing	
Bug Id	(Lines)	Comment Lines	Test Only	All Tests
#34925	79	0.89	0.48	0.48
#36803	7	0.43	0.14	0.14
#37739	4	0.75	0.75	0.75
#39993	178	0.80	0.49	0.49
#42993	63	0.97	0.02	0.02
#43033	5	1.00	0.80	0.80
#47754	7	0.86	0.29	0.29
#49457	11	1.00	0.64	0.64
#49638	6	1.00	1.00	1.00
#51320	43	0.91	0.67	0.67
#51322	6	0.83	0.67	0.67
#53981	8	0.25	0.12	0.12
#53999	4	1.00	0.50	0.50
#54421	27	1.00	0.59	0.59
#55341	1	1.00	1.00	1.00
#60015	5	0.80	0.60	0.60

Table 6.7: Minimization results for ASPECTJ (1/2). The remaining results can be found in Table 6.8.

			Minimization Results	
Bug Id	Size of Fix (Lines)	Fraction of Non-Comment Lines	Failing Test Only	All Tests
#61536	15	0.93	0.60	0.60
#62642	18	0.94	0.22	0.22
#64069	23	0.83	0.35	0.35
#64331	23	0.96	0.57	0.61
#65319	41	0.88	0.59	0.61
#67774	4	0.75	0.50	0.50
#68991	17	1.00	1.00	1.00
#69459	11	1.00	0.82	0.82
#70619	10	0.80	0.90	0.90
#71377	55	0.82	0.55	0.55
#72157	7	0.86	0.71	0.71
#72528	74	0.73	0.22	0.32
#72531	20	0.85	0.60	0.60
#76096	12	0.75	0.50	0.50
#80249	86	0.81	0.29	0.29
#87376	6	1.00	0.83	0.83
#173602	2	1.00	0.50	0.50
∅	**26**	**0.86**	**0.56**	**0.56**
~	**11**	**0.88**	**0.59**	**0.60**

Table 6.8: Minimization results for ASPECTJ (2/2). The median bug has 44% of irrelevant lines.

we conclude that the ASPECTJ team is more concerned with project quality than the RHINO developers. This is in line with observations made in Section 6.4.

Minimization Our minimization tool is able to identify irrelevant lines in 88% of all bugs in AS-PECTJ, and 80% of the bugs in RHINO. Thus we can conclude that the majority of commits classified as bug fixes contain changes that are irrelevant for fixing the bug. To measure the extent of the problem, we compare the fraction of lines deemed relevant for the fix to the fraction of non-comment lines (columns three and five in Tables 6.6 and 6.7): For both projects, DELTA DEBUGGING identifies roughly one third of the changed lines as irrelevant which is a considerable fraction. The discussion at the end of this section presents ideas how to reduce the amount of noise.

Test Function To evaluate the effect of including all tests in the test function, we compare median values from columns four and five. For RHINO, using only the failing test causes roughly one third of the median minimized fix more lines to be removed than when using all tests. We conclude that for RHINO it is very important to use the whole test suite in the test function. Otherwise, DELTA DEBUGGING identifies lines as irrelevant that are actually relevant for the correctness of the fix. In comparison, for for ASPECTJ the results are almost identical, indicating that the regression tests provided by the developers are of high quality. This confirms our previous observations that the ASPECTJ team puts more emphasis on project maintenance and test quality.

To validate the results of the minimization, we investigated a sample of the bugs included in the study. We chose bugs for which including all tests made a strong difference, and bugs that showed a large overall minimization. Since understanding the effects of a fix requires a lot of human effort, we restricted ourselves to a sample size of four bugs split evenly over both projects:

ASPECTJ #42993 & #80249 For both bugs, DELTA DEBUGGING is able to significantly reduce the number of lines. The fix for bug #42993 contains large blocks of changes that seem to deal with optimizations made by the compiler. These optimizations seem to have no influence on the remaining tests and therefore are deemed irrelevant. For bug #80249 the commit contains a number of changes that implement a new feature that is unrelated to the bug. These lines are removed by DELTA DEBUGGING.

RHINO #157509 & #203402 The fix for bug #157509 is concerned with parsing a number of special characters. The failing test only contains one of those characters. Hence, DELTA DEBUGGING removes the code for the remaining characters, when using only the failing run. However, other tests in the test suite contain more of the special characters and therefore DELTA DEBUGGING removes much fewer lines. In the case of bug #203402, one line of the fix replaces the values of variables with constants (see Figure 6.8). This line is identified as irrelevant by DELTA DEBUGGING as the failing run has the same values as the constants for the variables. Thus, the failing run actually is too imprecise to fully capture the effects of the bug.

```
1  <       generateCodeFromNode(child, node, trueLabel, falseLabel);
2  <       generateCodeFromNode(child.getNext(),
3  <                            node, trueLabel, falseLabel);
4  ---
5  >       generateCodeFromNode(child, node, -1, -1);
6  >       generateCodeFromNode(child.getNext(), node, -1, -1);
```

Figure 6.8: The fix for bug `203402`. If DELTA DEBUGGING only relies on the failing run, the first line is deemed irrelevant since the failing run has −1 for both `trueLabel` and `falseLabel`.

Overall, our manual investigation revealed no misclassified lines, which indicates that our implementation is correct and produces reliable results. In the next section, we discuss general threats to the validity of our results.

Threats to Validity

As any empirical evaluation, the results of our experiments are subject to threats to validity:

Threats to external validity concern our ability to generalize our results. The scope of our study is limited as it only includes 45 bugs of two different projects. Also, the way we selected bugs introduces a bias towards projects that use version archives, bug repositories and automated tests. Thus, we cannot claim that our results are generalizable to all projects.

Threats to internal validity concern our ability to draw conclusions about the connections between our independent and dependent variables. DDCHANGE, the implementation of DELTA DEBUGGING used in our experiments has been used in several different projects. Thus, we believe that it is sufficiently mature to be useful. However, it may still be the case that our implementation contains errors that affect the correctness of our results. To counter this threat, we have manually investigated a subset of the bugs and found no obvious errors.

Threats to construct validity concern the adequacy of our measures for capturing dependent variables. In our experiments, the sole dependent variable captured is the number of lines affected by the minimized fix. We believe that this is an adequate measure to capture the size of a fix. More fine-grained processing would allow to minimize a fix on lower levels of abstraction, for example on byte code level. However, we believe that using single lines as granularity is the best option, as many lines in a program represent logical entities (for example method calls, boolean queries) that should not be split further.

Conclusions

The results of our experiment show that for the investigated sample roughly 30% of the changed lines are not required to fix the bug. Due to the nature of our minimization technique, our sample is biased towards bugs with associated test cases. However, we make no requirements regarding the structure or the location of a fix. This gives us reason to believe that the ratio of irrelevant lines in our experiments is comparable to other bugs in the repository, and possibly also in other projects.

Overall, the ratio of irrelevant lines is considerable. The root cause is the imperfect heuristic to identify bug fixes, which is also used in other approaches [124]. The main conclusion of our results is that this technique should be used carefully and the results need to be analyzed carefully. For IBUGS, we have put our results online and advise researchers to only use the minimized fixes.

In the future, we need more reliable approaches to identify fixes in version archives. Possible ways to approach this problem include the following:

Manual Investigation One way to remove irrelevant lines is to manually minimize each potential fix. However, for large repositories and fixes, this clearly is too much effort.

Minimization Another option is to rely on minimization techniques as proposed in this section. However, since minimization requires an oracle, this approach always produces samples biased towards bugs with automated tests.

Explicit Linking The best solution would be to improve the development process such that linking no longer needs to rely on heuristics. For example, the JAZZ platform [43] provides means to explicitly link a bug report to a transaction in the version archive. However, it may still be the case that a developer misuses this feature, thereby creating spurious links that again introduce irrelevant changes.

The next section presents work by other researchers that compare IBUGS to similar bug data sets and investigate whether the sample of bugs contained in the repository is biased or not.

6.6 Biased Data Sets

IBUGS only includes a subset of all bugs that occurred in the history of each subject. This is due to several requirements a bug has to fulfill to qualify for the repository. For example, many bugs cannot be linked to transactions at all. Also, some bugs are not included because the source code of the revision cannot be compiled. As a consequence, the set of bugs in IBUGS is only a sample of all bugs. Hence, this sample may be *biased*, i.e. the bugs in the sample differ significantly from the remaining bugs. In that case, the results of an evaluation performed on the sample are not generalizable to all bugs in the subject. To judge the quality of IBUGS as a benchmark, we would like to know whether the sample of bugs for the subjects is biased or not.

Other researchers recognized the problem of biased samples in bug data sets. In recent work, Bird et al. [12] investigate the bias of several bug data sets mined from history, among them the ASPECTJ dataset. The results of their study give important insights on the quality of the ASPECTJ dataset, which is why we present a summary of their findings in the following sections.

6.6.1 Bug Features

To evaluate whether a bug benchmark is biased, Bird et al. compare the set of bugs included in a benchmark to all bugs available for the program. To be able to compare bugs, Bird et al. introduce a set of *bug features* that measure different aspects of both the development process and the bug itself. These features are then used to compare the sample of each subject against the whole set of bugs.

The whole set of bugs available for a subject s is denoted as B. The set of bugs included in the dataset for a subject is denoted as B_i. Obviously, B_i is a subset of B. The question is whether B_i is a representative subset of the bugs in B. To investigate this, Bird et al. compare the distribution of several *bug features* in B and B_i. If B_i is a representative sample of B, there should be no statistically significant differences in the two distributions.

For the bugs in $B \cap B_i$, the fix is unknown. The selection of bug features therefore has to be restricted to features that are known for all bugs. In their work, Bird et al. examine the following features:

Severity is a feature that classifies the importance of a bug. Developers assign a severity level as soon as a bug is confirmed. Typical values for severity levels are `blocker`, `minor` and `trivial`. Bird et al. argue that the severity level is an important bug feature because developers are more interested in fixing severe bugs. Hence, the sample set B_i should contain the same proportion of severe bugs as found in B.

Experience measures a developer's background in fixing bugs. Bird et al. approximate experience of a developer d at time t as the number of bugs d fixed prior to t.

Verification is a binomial variable indicating whether or not a bug is verified after it has been resolved. This feature captures the process a bug goes through. Severe bugs generally receive more attention and hence are more likely to be verified.

To gather the data required to measure these features, Bird et al. use publicly available bug databases for all benchmark subjects included in the study. In their study, Bird et al. examine two variants of the ECLIPSE dataset [124], the ASPECTJ subject of IBUGS, and four additional projects for which they use their own tool to identify fixes. The left part of Table 6.9 shows the total number of bugs and the number of linked bugs for all projects. In this setting ASPECTJ is the smallest subject in terms of the number of bugs.

6.6.2 Results

To evaluate whether the bugs in B_i differ from those in B, Bird et al. formulate the following three hypotheses based on the bug features introduced above:

Severity There is a difference in the distribution of severity levels between B and B_i.

Experience Bugs in B_i are fixed by more experienced people than those who fix bugs in B.

Verified Bugs in B_i are more likely to have been verified than the population of B.

For every subject, Bird et al. test each of the three hypotheses. In order for a subject to be unbiased, all three hypotheses need to be *rejected*. The results of the evaluation are summarized in columns

			Hypotheses		
Subject	Total Bugs	Linked Bugs	Severity	Experience	Verified
ECLIPSE-B	24 119	10 017	✓	✓	✓
ECLIPSE-Z	113 877	34 919	✓	✓	✓
APACHE	1383	686	✓	✓	✠
NETBEANS	68 299	37 498	N/A	✓	✓
OPENOFFICE	33 924	2754	N/A	✓	✓
GNOME	117 021	45 527	✓	✓	✠
ASPECTJ	1121	343	✠	✠	✠

Table 6.9: Subjects used in the bias evaluation presented by Bird et al. [12]. The right side shows evaluation results for different hypotheses. Each entry lists whether a hypothesis for a subject was accepted (✓) or rejected (✠).

"Severity", "Experience" and "Verified" of Table 6.9. Each entry lists whether a hypothesis for a subject was accepted (✓) or rejected (✠). In two cases (marked as N/A), the subjects did not provide severity data and hence the hypotheses could not be evaluated.

The results show that for ASPECTJ, all three hypotheses were rejected. This means that there is no statistically significant difference between bugs in B and B_i in terms of severity, experience of developers and verification status. In contrast, all of the other five subjects showed a strong bias for at least two of the investigated features. Bird et al. summarize:

> The conclusion from this in-depth analysis is that there is no bias in the IBUGS ASPECTJ data set with regard to the bug features examined. This is an encouraging result, in that it gives us a concrete data set that lacks bias (along the dimensions we tested).

6.7 Conclusions

The version history of a project collects all past successes and failures. In this section we presented IBUGS, an approach that leverages the history of a project to automatically extract benchmarks for bug localization tools. We have applied our approach to two different projects and mined a total of over 380 bugs. In contrast to similar repositories, IBUGS also identifies tests associated with a fix, and provides an infrastructure to execute the test suite in each revision. Thus, IBUGS is useful for both static and dynamic approaches that want to perform an evaluation using realistic bug data.

IBUGS makes several assumptions about the structure of commits and log messages and uses heuristics to identify fixes. Due to these assumptions, IBUGS sometimes incorrectly classifies changes (or parts of a commit) as fixes. To investigate the extent of this issue, we have implemented a minimization algorithm that relies on associated tests and the test suite to identify irrelevant changes. In our experiments, roughly one third of the lines changed by 48 fixes in two projects are irrelevant, which is a considerable amount of noise. In the absence of a more reliable technique to identify fixes, we recommend using minimized fixes obtained by running DELTA DEBUGGING on a subset of the bugs in IBUGS.

Despite this problem we believe that IBUGS can be of great value to the research community. The bugs collected by IBUGS are real bugs as they occur in real projects. Also, work by other researchers [12] shows that the ASPECTJ subject is the only dataset that contains an unbiased sample of bugs. Therefore, results obtained by using IBUGS are more likely to transfer to real projects than results obtained from other repositories such as SIR [37] or the ECLIPSE PROMISE dataset [124].

To allow other researchers to benefit from our work, the dataset is publicly available. In addition, we also provide a fully-fledged infrastructure for reconstructing, building, and testing the versions with and without bugs (see the step-by-step guide in Figure A.1 on page 138).

The IBUGS dataset is a first step towards the "huge collection of software bugs" that was demanded by Spacco et al. [96] at the Bugs workshop at PLDI 2005. The history of open source projects offer a huge number of bugs which wait to be discovered by researchers.

Chapter 7

Mining Models for Typestate Verification

In the last decade, we have witnessed a tremendous increase in the amount and the quality of available open source software. There are hundreds of thousands [1] of open-source projects, many of which offer well-tested libraries. Such projects are of interest to project managers, since they can help a project avoid reinventing the wheel. The downside of using third-party libraries is that it often requires a considerable amount of effort to learn the correct usage. Some classes have a rather complex interface, which makes them easy to misuse.

To avoid bugs due to incorrect usage of classes, researchers have devised a number of different techniques. One well-known approach is called *typestate verification*, which statically verifies that the usage of a class C can not raise an exception at runtime. To verify a class C, the typestate verifier requires a *typestate automaton* for C, which relates transitions in the state of C to method calls. In particular, a typestate automaton contains special transitions for method invocations that raise exceptions. Recent approaches for typestate verification [40] are able to analyze projects with up to four thousand methods in minutes. In a few years, typestate verification will be fast enough to be built into modern IDEs.

Unfortunately, almost no projects provide typestate automata (or any other form of machine-readable specification). However, many of them have executable usage examples, for instance in the form of a regression test suite or example programs. In this chapter, we investigate the usage of object behavior models as input to a static typestate verifier. If mined from a regression test suite, object behavior models can make previously hidden usage rules explicit and provide them in a format suitable for a typestate verifier. Since both approaches are based on finite state automata, converting object behavior models into typestate automata is straightforward.

Unfortunately, in practice, most regression test suites do not provide enough coverage to produce meaningful and complete automata. The reason is that most developers only test core functionality with positive usage examples. Only few test suites also provide tests for negative examples that trigger exceptions, and they usually do not explore all statically possible ways to use a class. However, to mine typestate automata it is vital to have good coverage and tests that trigger exceptions. Otherwise, the verifier may produce too many false positives and miss calls that cause exceptions.

To solve this problem, we propose to use *test case generation* to explore new behavior and enrich

---

[1] To date, Sourceforge.net (the biggest open-source project hoster) hosts over 230 000 projects.

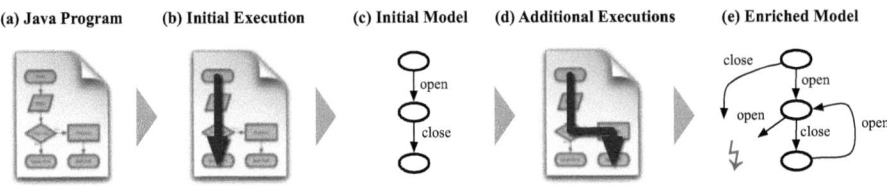

Figure 7.1: TAUTOKO overview. TAUTOKO takes an executable JAVA program (a) and observes its execution (b) to extract an initial typestate model (c). It then generates additional executions (test cases) to cover missing model transitions (d). The additional observed behavior results in an enriched specification (e).

existing specifications. We have implemented our approach in a tool called TAUTOKO [2], which builds upon the ADABU tool presented in the previous section. Our approach is as follows (see Figure 7.1): First, we use ADABU to mine object behavior models from the execution of regression test suites. The initially mined model contains only observed transitions (Section 7.2). To enrich the specification, our TAUTOKO tool generates test cases to cover all possible transitions between all observed states, and thus extracts *additional transitions* from their executions (Section 7.3). These transitions can either end in legal states, thus indicating additional legal interaction; or they can raise an *exception*, thus indicating illegal interaction. Discovering such illegal interactions is the biggest advantage of our approach, as exceptional behavior is rarely covered by conventional executions or tests.

To assess the benefits of enriched specifications, we put them to use in static typestate verification. The success of typestate verification depends on the *completeness of the given model:* The more transitions are known as illegal, the more bugs can be reported; and the more transitions are known as legal, the more likely it is that additional transitions can be treated as illegal. We expect that our enriched specifications are much closer to completeness than the initially mined specifications; and therefore, the static verifier should be much more accurate in its reports.

This hypothesis is confirmed by an experiment (Section 7.4): On a sample of 800 bugs seeded into six Java subjects, we show that our static typestate verifier fed with enriched models reports significantly more true positives, and significantly less false positives than when being fed with the initial models.[3]

To show that object behavior models can actually help developers to avoid misusing classes, we have developed a plugin for ECLIPSE that runs typestate analysis whenever the developer saves a new version of a file.

In the remainder of this chapter, we introduce the typestate miner (Section 7.2), explain our technique for test case generation (Section 7.3), present the results of our evaluation (Section 7.4), discuss related work (Section 7.5) and conclude with a summary and ideas for future work (Section 7.6).

Parts of this chapter are accepted for publication at the 2010 International Symposium on Software Testing and Analysis [27].

---

[2] "Tautoko" is the Māori word for "enhance, enrich".
[3] In the remainder of this chapter, we will use the terms "specification" and "model" interchangeably.

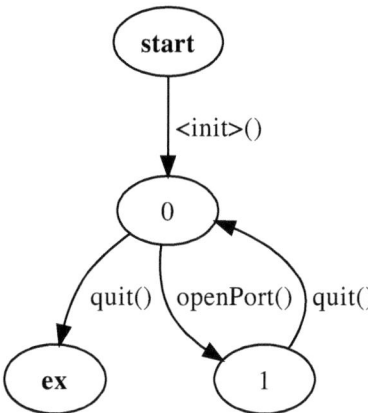

Figure 7.2: Typestate for `SMTPProtocol`. The failing call to `quit()` shows as a transition to *ex*.

7.1 Typestate Analysis

The term *typestate* was introduced by Strom et al. [99]. In object-oriented languages, the *type* of an object encompasses the set of all methods that can be invoked on the object. In contrast, the typestate enables only a subset of all operations based on the current state of the object. Transitions between states occur by invoking *enabled methods*, possibly enabling a different set of methods. Whenever a *disabled method* is invoked, an error occurs and the typestate switches to an *error state*.

A *typestate automaton* (or simply typestate) is a finite state automaton which encodes the typestate sequence of a class. Figure 7.2 shows an example typestate automaton for the `SMTPProtocol` class from the ristretto [35] library. After initialization, an `SMTPProtocol` object is in its initial state 0; calling `openPort()` brings it into state 1; and calling `quit()` from this state brings it back into the initial state 0.

As explained above, invoking a method *m* that is disabled according to the typestate automaton causes a transition labeled with *m* to a special state *ex*. In our example, this is the case if `quit()` is invoked from the initial state 0, which raises a `NullPointerException`. A static typestate verifier can take this very specification and check a client for conformance; if it is possible to invoke `quit()` while still being in the initial state 0, the verifier will flag an error.

7.2 Mining Typestate Automata

How can we mine typestate automata from program executions? When comparing them to object behavior models, we immediately see that they are closely related. Both types of models are finite state automata where transitions are labeled with the names of methods. The only differences between them are the way states are identified, and the representation of exceptions:

States In typestate automata, states do not have a label; in object behavior models, they are labeled with the values of fields and inspector methods.

Exceptions Typestates represent failing method calls by transitions to a special state *ex*. In object behavior models, information about exceptions is stored as meta data in the transition labels.

In a sense, a typestate automaton is simply an object behavior model with unlabeled states. Hence, an algorithm to convert behavior models into typestate automata is straightforward and essentially consists of the following three steps:

1. The automaton is initialized with two states labeled *start* and *ex*.

2. Each state *s* of the behavior model is assigned a unique number *n*, and a corresponding state labeled *n* is added to the typestate.

3. For each invocation of a method *m* between two states s_i and s_j, a new transition labeled with *m* is added to the typestate: If the invocation raised an exception, the transition is added from s_i to *ex*, otherwise it is added from s_i to s_j.

With this conversion algorithm, we can use ADABU to mine object behavior models, and afterwards convert them to typestate automata.

7.3 Enriching Typestate Automata

To yield precise results and few false positives during verification, a typestate needs to be *complete*, i.e. it needs to contain all relevant states and transitions for all methods in all states. When we first began our work, we ran TAUTOKO on a set of projects and mined typestates from the test suite executions for a set of interesting classes. Unfortunately, for the investigated classes, we found that most typestates only contained a fraction of all transitions. In particular, most typestates were missing transitions for failing methods, which renders mined typestates useless for typestate verification.

We believe that the lack of observed failures is an issue that is common to many projects—and thus affects every approach for dynamic specification mining:

- Most bugs due to wrong usage of a class raise exceptions and are therefore easy to detect and fix. Thus, a specification miner will seldom record misuse and exceptions when tracing normal application executions.

- Unfortunately, we observed the same problem of missing exceptions when tracing test suites. Most developers do not test for exceptions. One explanation for this is that triggering an exception often only covers a few lines, and hence developers concentrate on tests for normal behavior.

- To generate a complete model, lots of tests are required. Usually, developers do not have enough time to write so many tests. Also, developers tend to skip tests which they consider to be too obvious or are convinced that they should work.

7.3. ENRICHING TYPESTATE AUTOMATA

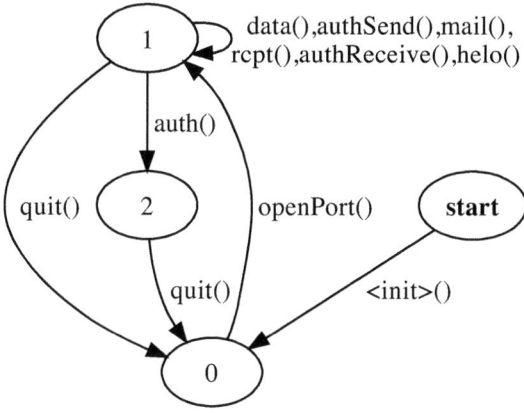

Figure 7.3: Initial model of the SMTPProtocol class.

One way to approach this problem is to use test case generation to create new tests that execute previously unknown states and transitions. The general idea of combining specification mining with test case generation was first described by Xie and Notkin [114]. In this work, we extend the original idea to generate tests specifically targeted at enriching typestate automata. There is a huge variety of test generation strategies, ranging from complex static analyzes such as symbolic execution [104] to simple random testing techniques [21, 75]. In this work, we use a test generation strategy that generates new tests by *mutating an existing test suite*.

Our technique works as follows: In the first step, TAUTOKO executes the test suite and mines a model for the class under test (CUT). This model is called the *initial model*. After that, it attempts to generate mutations to the test suite such that all methods are executed in all states of the initial model. TAUTOKO then applies each mutant in isolation and mines new models from the execution of the modified test suite. Finally, the initial model and all new models are combined into the model for the CUT.

To demonstrate the effect of TAUTOKO, consider Figure 7.3 which shows the initial model of class SMTPProtocol mined from an execution of the project's test suite. In contrast, Figure 7.4 shows the enriched model generated by TAUTOKO after evaluating all mutations. Not only does the enriched model contain several additional transitions, but it now also explicitly lists the exceptional behavior in its ex state. We will use these models to illustrate the techniques presented in this section.

Mutant generation starts by statically determining the set of methods that belong to the CUT or one of its super types. For every such method m, TAUTOKO tries to generate mutations such that m is invoked in all states of the initial model. To invoke method m in state s, TAUTOKO will either add an invocation of m, or suppress one or more existing method invocations. The choice of adding or deleting invocations depends on the number and types of the parameters m expects.

If m only requires a reference to the receiver object, TAUTOKO simply adds a new call to m right after a method call that caused a transition to s in the initial model. For example, in Figure 7.3, to

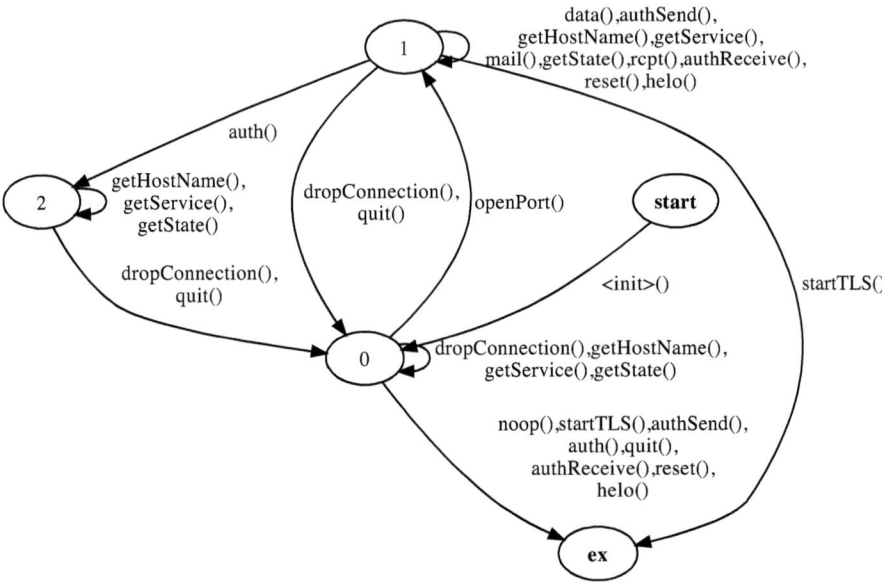

Figure 7.4: Enriched model of the SMTPProtocol class. Compare with the initial model in Figure 7.3.

invoke method dropConnection() in state 1, TAUTOKO adds a call to dropConnection() right after the call to openPort() that causes the transition to state 1.

A problem arises if *m* expects parameters beyond the receiver object. In this case, we need to provide values for the parameters in order to call *m*. Our approach is to *reuse existing invocations* of *m*. If the initial model contains an invocation of *m* in another state *t*, TAUTOKO suppresses method calls such that the call occurs in state *s* instead. For example, to call method authSend(byte[]) in state 0, we can suppress the invocation of openPort() that causes the transition from state 0 to 1.

The advantage of this approach is that it is simple to implement and works also for complex parameters that are difficult to generate. However, our approach is unable to handle methods with parameters that are never invoked by the program. To call such methods, we would need more generic test generation schemes [75, 103]. Still, our evaluation results show that even with this simple approach, enriched specifications already contain much more information and are likely to be much more useful in any verification setting.

Algorithm 2 shows pseudo code for the procedure to enrich a typestate for class *c*. Input to the algorithm consists of the test suite, the initial typestate and the set of methods that can be called on *c*. The main loop of the algorithm (lines 3-23) iterates over all states *s* of the initial typestate. For every method *m* that expects parameters other than the receiver (lines 7-14), TAUTOKO finds all invocations of *m* in the initial typestate (line 8), tries to find a path that leads to *s*, and creates a mutated test that suppresses all method calls along the path (line 12). If the sole parameter to *m* is the receiver (lines

Subject	Type	Description
javamail	`SMTPTransport`	Sending mails via SMTP.
javax.security	`LoginModule`	User authentication.
ristretto	`SMTPProtocol`	Sending mails via SMTP.
signature	`Signature`	Handling of digital signatures.
socket	`Socket`	Network communication.
zip	`ZipOutputStream`	File compression with zip algorithm.

Table 7.1: Subjects used in the case studies. The first three subjects are publicly available libraries, whereas the remaining classes are part of the JAVA standard API.

16-20), TAUTOKO finds all transitions after which the object is in state s (line 16) and generates a new test that invokes m right after the call that caused the transition (line 18). The final loop (lines 25-28) executes all tests, mines new typestates from each execution, and merges the new typestate into the current version. After the loop has finished, the procedure returns the enriched typestate.

7.4 Experimental Evaluation

In this section, we investigate how well TAUTOKO works in practice. Our goal is to compare the usefulness of *enriched models* versus *initial models* as well as manually generated *complete models*, and thus investigate the benefits and potential drawbacks of our approach.

7.4.1 Subjects

To evaluate the effectiveness of TAUTOKO, we have applied it to six different JAVA subjects listed in Table 7.1. Altogether, we chose 6 different classes for which we generated and evaluated typestate automata. Three classes (upper half in Table 7.1) are part of publicly available libraries, whereas the remaining classes are part of the JAVA standard API. In terms of domain, we can divide the subjects into *security* (`javax.security` and `signature`) related and *I/O* (`javamail`, `ristretto`, `socket` and `zip`) related.

We chose our subjects by investigating a subset of open-source projects from big hosting sites such as `Sourceforge` and `java.net`, as well as classes from the JAVA standard API. We included subjects that met the following criteria:

1. The API documentation of the class explicitly or implicitly mentions *restrictions on the order of method invocation*. In other words, we made sure that our subjects are complex enough to yield interesting specifications.

2. As a source for test runs, we solely rely on *executions as provided* by the developers of the subject class. This is to avoid introducing additional bias with self-constructed test-cases. For the first three subjects in Table 7.1, we use sample executions and regression test suites provided

Algorithm 2 Enrich Typestate Automaton

Input: Test Suite $T = (t_1, \ldots, t_n)$
Input: Initial typestate $M_{init} = (V_{init}, E_{init})$
Input: Methods to investigate M
Output: Enriched Typestate $M_{final} = (V_{final}, E_{final})$

1: **procedure** ENRICH(T,M_{init})
2: $\quad T' = \{\}$
3: $\quad$ **for all** $s \in V_{init} \setminus \{\text{start}\}$ **do**
4: $\quad\quad M_s \leftarrow \{\text{Methods invoked in } s\}$
5: $\quad\quad$ **for all** $m \in \{M \setminus M_s\}$ **do**
6: $\quad\quad\quad$ **if** hasParameters(m) **then**
7: $\quad\quad\quad\quad S_m \leftarrow \{s \in V_{init} \mid \exists (s, s', n) \in E_{init} : m = n\}$
8: $\quad\quad\quad\quad$ **for all** $u \in S_m$ **do**
9: $\quad\quad\quad\quad\quad p \leftarrow \text{getPath}(u, s)$
10: $\quad\quad\quad\quad\quad$ **if** length(p) $< \infty$ **then**
11: $\quad\quad\quad\quad\quad\quad T'.\text{add}(\text{suppressAllCalls}(T, p))$
12: $\quad\quad\quad\quad\quad$ **end if**
13: $\quad\quad\quad\quad$ **end for**
14: $\quad\quad\quad$ **else**
15: $\quad\quad\quad\quad T_s \leftarrow \{(s, s', n) \in E_{init}\}$
16: $\quad\quad\quad\quad$ **for all** $t \in T_s$ **do**
17: $\quad\quad\quad\quad\quad T'.\text{add}(\text{addCall}(T, t, m))$
18: $\quad\quad\quad\quad$ **end for**
19: $\quad\quad\quad$ **end if**
20: $\quad\quad$ **end for**
21: $\quad$ **end for**
22: $\quad M_{final} \leftarrow M_{init}$
23: $\quad$ **for all** $t \in T'$ **do**
24: $\quad\quad M_{new} \leftarrow \text{run}(t)$
25: $\quad\quad M_{final} \leftarrow \text{merge}(M_{new}, M_{final})$
26: $\quad$ **end for**
27: **end procedure**

by the respective projects. We made sure that these runs cover all essential methods of the subject class. For the JAVA standard classes in our evaluation, we use conformance tests of the APACHE HARMONY project. This project aims at providing an open-source alternative to the JAVA standard classes, and therefore has a sophisticated test suite to ensure compliance with the original implementation by SUN.

3. To conduct the evaluation using the static typestate verifier, we needed an additional application for each subject that uses the subject class in its implementation. To find such applications, we searched the web using `koders.com` and `google code` search engines. To qualify for our evaluation, a project had to offer a minimum level of maturity and provide a test run that executes the subject class (See Section 7.4.4 for a rationale).

We are aware that our selection process creates a bias towards complex classes and well-tested projects. However, the purpose of this evaluation is not to evaluate the usage of mined specifications in general. Instead, we study how our approach for enriching mined specifications improves quality and applicability of the specifications. Section 7.4.5 provides a detailed discussion of threats to the validity of our results.

7.4.2 Quantitative Evaluation

In this section, we provide a *quantitative evaluation* of our technique for enriching mined specifications. For every subject, we mine an initial model (see Section 7.2) from the execution of the test suite. Afterward, we use TAUTOKO to mutate the test suite and mine an enriched model. To quantify the difference between the two versions, we count the number of states and the number of transitions. A transition in this context means a method call. Since we are mostly interested in *exceptional* behavior, we also measure the number of exceptional transitions. The results of the quantitative evaluation are summarized in Table 7.2.

For `SMTPProtocol`, we also provided the initial model in Figure 7.3 and the enriched version in Figure 7.4[4]. Both versions have the same number of states. However, the enriched version has about three times as many transitions. Also, the initial model has no exceptional transitions, compared to 9 transitions in the enriched version.

Applied to all subjects, TAUTOKO discovers new states for three out of six subjects, and significantly increases the number of transitions for all of them. None of the initial models for the first three subjects has exceptional transitions, hinting at a low quality of the test suite. This is a general trend we observed in many projects, as discussed earlier. For each of those subjects, TAUTOKO discovers new transitions that trigger exceptions. Initial models for the JAVA API classes already contain transitions to the error state. Obviously, the conformance tests of the HARMONY project also test for expected negative behavior. For the API subjects, TAUTOKO significantly increases the number of both exceptional and normal transitions. The largest relative increase is observed for `socket`, with a total of 55 exceptional transitions compared to only 2 in the initial model.

---
[4]Models for the remaining subjects are available online at the website given in Section 7.6.

		Original model			Enriched model		
			Transitions			Transitions	
Subject	Mutations	States	Regular	Fail	States	Regular	Fail
javamail	61	6	5	0	13	48	2
javax.security	9	6	5	0	6	14	6
ristretto	55	5	11	0	5	33	9
signature	23	5	30	8	5	39	13
socket	540	11	35	2	17	251	55
zip	145	11	24	5	14	62	18

Table 7.2: Results of the quantitative evaluation. Column "Fail" gives the number of transitions that raise an exception. Overall, enriched models have more transitions, and many more exceptional transitions.

		Transitions	
Subject	States	Regular	Fail
ristretto	7	86	29
signature	5	48	12
zip	6	31	9

Table 7.3: Manually specified typestate models.

Overall, applying TAUTOKO leads to larger models with significantly more transitions. In the next section, we investigate if TAUTOKO also improves the quality of the mined specifications.

7.4.3 Qualitative Evaluation

In this section, we take a look at how well the initial and enriched models reflect the *complete model* of the class. To this end, we compared the mined models with complete usage models. Since there are no models available for our subjects, we had to manually create them. To create the models, we investigated the source code to build a mental model that was translated into a typestate. In a few cases it was difficult to reliably judge if a method could be called in a certain state. To clarify those cases, we wrote small test cases that resolved the issue.

One problem with manual model generation is how to deal with unchecked exceptions. In JAVA, many instructions may cause null pointer dereferences or illegal array accesses. Including transitions for all those exceptions would introduce a high degree of non-determinism, which essentially renders the model useless. We therefore only include transitions for checked exceptions.

Manually creating models involves a lot of human effort (which, of course, is why we wanted to build TAUTOKO in the first place). We therefore restricted our evaluation to only three subjects, namely SMTPProtocol, ZipOutputStream and Signature. In total, we spent over 10 hours on creating the specifications, where most of the time was spent on SMTPProtocol, which is also the most complex. Unfortunately, the models are too large to depict them in this thesis. However, they are available for download at the address given in Chapter 9. Table 7.3 lists structural details of the manually mined models.

To investigate whether TAUTOKO also improves the quality of the mined specifications, we compared initial and enriched models against the complete model:

ristretto The complete model has two more states than the initial and the enriched models. The two additional states are related to sending mails, which requires a call to initiate the mail, followed by several calls to set receivers, and a final call to send the mail. No state-based specification miner can detect this protocol, since relevant state information is transmitted to the server and is not kept locally. Apart from this, all states and transitions of the initial model are also reflected in the complete model.

The enriched model adds twenty valid transitions and nine exceptional transitions. Two exceptional transitions are invalid according to the complete model. They are caused by limitations of the mock server, which is used in the test suite of SMTPProtocol. This shows a limitation of our completion technique: TAUTOKO may break the boundaries of the test suite and generate invalid transitions.

signature The initial and the enriched models have the same number of states. All transitions in the initial model are in accordance with the complete model. TAUTOKO adds nine additional transitions, five out of which are exceptional transitions. All transitions are also reflected in the complete model. In total, the enriched model misses six transitions. This is due to the way TAUTOKO injects and suppresses method calls, which prevents some methods from being called in certain states.

zip The complete model has much fewer states than both the initial and the enriched model. This occurs because states in the model miner also include values for fields that are irrelevant for the usage of the object, such as fields comment or method. The initial model essentially contains the structure of the complete model twice, once with method set and once without. The enriched model contains additional states with comments. Despite the blow-up, the mined models are still useful since they capture all exceptional transitions of the complete model.

In summary, we found that the specification miner in combination with TAUTOKO generates valid specifications compared to manually deduced models. Like any test case generation technique, TAUTOKO cannot guarantee to cover all possible transitions; and this limitation also holds for the present subjects. Section 7.6 presents ideas for future work to improve coverage. In one case, TAUTOKO generates transitions that do not match the complete model. This is due to restrictions which are inherent to the general technique of enriching models by manipulating an existing test suite.

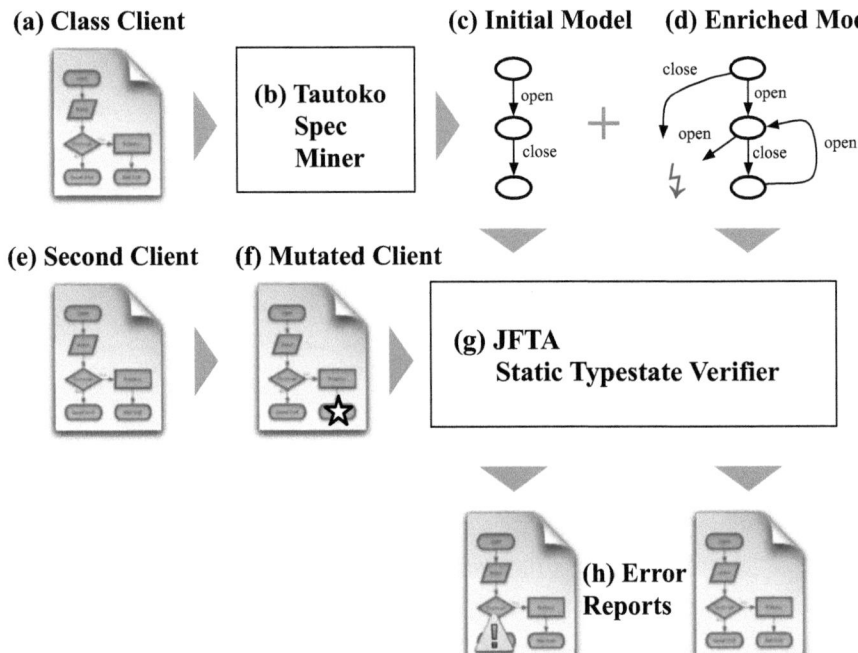

Figure 7.5: Evaluation overview. We take the client (a) of a class and use TAUTOKO (b) to mine both the initial model (c) and the enriched model (d). We then take a second client (e) of the same class and seed in a bug (f). The JFTA (see Section 7.4.4) static typestate verifier (g) then produces error reports (h) for the mutated client using both the initial model and the enriched model. Were available, we also include complete models (see Section 7.4.3). We compare the error reports in terms of true positives and false positives.

7.4.4 Usefulness

Results of the previous sections show that applying TAUTOKO yields better specifications. However, we would also like to know if this improvement matters in practice. To investigate this, we ran a *static typestate verifier* on a set of randomly generated bugs and compared the results for initial and enriched models. For `ristretto`, `signature` and `zip`, we also included complete models from the previous section. The evaluation setting is summarized in Figure 7.5 and detailed in the following sections.

Experimental setting

Our experiment assumes the following situation: A developer starts building an application and uses classes from a library l for the first time. To help the developer avoid bugs due to incorrect usage of those classes, the IDE supports lightweight typestate verification. Whenever the developer changes a method that uses classes of l for which a specification is available, the IDE launches the typestate verifier. The verifier then analyzes all changed methods and looks for incorrect usage of classes; if it finds a violation, it is presented to the user. Obviously, we would like to catch as many bugs (true positives) and report as few false alarms (false positives) as possible.

To simulate the above situation in a controlled experiment, we take the following steps:

1. For each subject used in the evaluation so far, we find an *application* that uses the subject. We also require the application to provide a test suite or other means to execute the program.

2. We use our mutation tool to simulate changes a developer might make to the application. To this end, we generate *mutants* that randomly inject or suppress method calls to instances of the subject class in the application.

3. For each mutated version, we execute the *test suite* of the application to classify mutants. Mutants that raise an exception at runtime are bugs that we would like a typestate verifier to detect. Mutants that do not raise an exception use the class correctly, and therefore the verifier should not report a warning.

4. Finally, we run the verifier for each mutated version to analyze all methods touched by the mutant and remember all reported violations. We use the generated mutants to measure how often the verifier points to a method invocation that actually triggers an exception (true positive), and how often the verifier reports a violation although the program runs without producing an error (false positive).

The purpose of this experiment is to measure the effect of using enriched specifications as generated by TAUTOKO over using initial specifications produced by the test suite. We therefore repeat step 4 with initial models generated by the test suite and enriched models generated by TAUTOKO. For three subjects, we also include results for the complete models created for the qualitative evaluation of Section 7.4.3.

We ran our evaluation for the same set of subjects used for the previous experiments. Table 7.4 lists the test sources for generating models, as well as the names of all applications used in the evaluation.

Subject	Test Source	# Tests	Application
javamail	Regression test suite	6	JVerify Binary Verifier
javax.security	Regression test suite	5	Apache Jackrabbit
ristretto	Regression test suite	5	Fin J2EE calendar server
signature	Harmony compliance tests	16	opensc project
socket	Harmony compliance tests	5	CRSMail Server
zip	Harmony compliance tests	9	Huf 3.0

Table 7.4: Details about where tests came from and which applications were tested.

The JFTA Static Typestate Verifier

Unfortunately, existing typestate verifiers are either not released [40], or require additional input [10]. We have therefore implemented our own typestate verifier called JFTA. JFTA is a partially interprocedural, flow- and context-sensitive typestate verifier for JAVA classes. Input to JFTA consists of the program's byte code, a set of typestate automata, and a set of methods which are to be analyzed. In contrast to other tools such as Plural [10], JFTA does not require the programmer to provide annotations of the program code.

The core part of JFTA consists of a conservative dataflow analysis algorithm. Aliasing information is calculated using a demand-driven points-to analysis [98]. As the primary focus of JFTA is to execute quickly, the implementation uses several heuristics that trade precision for speed:

- When analyzing a method, JFTA only follows method calls up to a certain (configurable) depth. Thus, the analysis may miss method calls which potentially causes false positives or negatives.

- Information of different paths through a method is merged together. Thus, the analysis is path insensitive, which may cause false positives.

- Whenever the analysis is unable to determine the state of an object, it simply assumes that the object can be in any possible state. This may again generate false positives.

Due to the above heuristics, our approach is less precise than other tools such as the approach presented by Fink et al. [40]. However, in our setting we are interested in the effect of using enriched specifications rather than in absolute precision; and our results thus are likely to generalize to all sorts of typestate verifiers. This is further discussed in Section 7.4.5.

Results: True Positives

Table 7.5 summarizes the results for all changes that trigger exceptions. The six columns list results using initial, enriched and complete models where available. Column *Flagged* lists the number of bugs for which the verifier flags a violation. *Actual* gives the number of cases where the reported method call exactly matches the call that raises the exception. For all numbers of reported errors, higher values are better.

		Initial model		Enriched model		Complete model	
Subject	Bugs	Flagged	Actual	Flagged	Actual	Flagged	Actual
javamail	5	0	0	4	3	n/a	n/a
javax.security	3	0	0	2	1	n/a	n/a
ristretto	28	0	0	25	15	21	19
signature	12	6	4	12	10	12	10
socket	49	2	2	48	47	n/a	n/a
zip	23	19	14	19	18	22	19

Table 7.5: Enriched models show more true positives.

The results show that, when using enriched models, the verifier pinpoints more violations than with the initial versions. For the first three subjects, initial models cannot point to bugs since they do not contain exceptional transitions. For the remaining three subjects, initial models also detect violations. For signature and socket, enriched models detect considerably more violations. For zip, both versions report violations for the same number of changes. However, enriched models more frequently point to the method call that raises the exception.

Better performance of enriched models in finding violations comes as no big surprise, as they include many more exceptional transitions than initial models. Still, the increase is considerable and the difference is statistically significant according to a paired-t-test with p=0.05.

For zip and signature, complete models yield slightly better results than enriched models. Thus for those two cases, models enriched by TAUTOKO are almost as good as manually created specifications. However, for ristretto complete models find 4 more bugs (19 compared to 15). This is due to the nature of the typestate miner, which relies on the values of fields to capture an object's state (see Section 7.4.3). Even when using complete models, the verifier does not catch all bugs. This is due to technical limitations of JFTA, such as the limited call stack depth.

subsubsectionResults: False Positives

Apart from finding errors, we would also like to have as few false positives as possible. To investigate the false positive rate of initial and enriched models, we repeated the above experiment with *changes that did not cause exceptions.*[5] For those changes, the verifier should not output violations.

The results of this experiment are shown in Table 7.6. The columns "Initial" and "Enriched" list the number of false positives for all types of models. For javamail and signature, we observe significantly fewer false positives. For the remaining subjects, the difference is smaller, but enriched models generally produce fewer false positives. A paired-t-test yields a p-value of 0.0124, which tells us that enriched models produce statistically significantly fewer false positives than initial models.

Using complete models again yields the biggest improvement for ristretto with only seven false positives remaining. For the other two subjects, using manually created models provides no benefits over using enriched models from TAUTOKO.

---

[5] We used coverage analysis to make sure that each change is actually covered.

		Models		
Subject	Changes	Initial	Enriched	Complete
javamail	28	26	2	n/a
javax.security	4	4	2	n/a
ristretto	53	53	47	7
signature	29	12	0	0
socket	460	300	283	n/a
zip	30	26	18	15

Table 7.6: Enriched models show fewer false positives.

7.4.5 Threats to Validity

As any empirical study, the results of our experiments are subject to threats to validity. We distinguish between threats to internal, external, and construct validity:

Threats to *external validity* concern our ability to generalize the results of our study. We cannot claim that the results of our experimental evaluation are generalizable. Our sample size is small; in total we investigate six subjects in twelve different applications. Also, our choice of subjects is biased towards more complex classes of projects with executable regression test suites. Less complex classes tend to generate only trivial models, and therefore TAUTOKO is unlikely to enrich them. However, applying TAUTOKO on such classes would not cause any harm, since the enriched model always contains the initial model. In practice, though, only specifications for classes that are complex enough to be misused should be distributed.

Threats to *internal validity* concern our ability to draw conclusions about the connections between our independent and dependent variables. Our process of manually creating complete models in Section 7.4.3 may be subject to errors or bias. When creating the models, we may have unintentionally left out states or transitions, which may influence our results. We therefore have used test cases to distinguish ambiguities wherever necessary. In addition, we make the models available at our website so that other researchers can investigate them (see Section 7.6).

Threats to *construct validity* concern the adequacy of our measures for capturing dependent variables. The last experiment uses our typestate verifier to compare models in terms of their ability to detect errors. A potential problem exists because the typestate verifier may miss violations due to over approximations or technical limitations. We may therefore be unable to measure the number of correctly identified violations for a specification. However, our evaluation uses the same set of changes for both types of models. If over-approximations prevent the verifier from detecting a violation, it will do so for both types. As our evaluation focuses on the increase (or decrease for false positives), we believe that this is no real threat for the results of this experiment.

7.5 Related Work

The idea of combining test case generation with specification mining was conceived by Xie and Notkin [114]. They present a generic *feedback loop* framework where specifications are fed into a test case generator, the generated tests are used to refine the specifications, and the refined specifications are again given as input to the test case generator. We extend this work by providing an implementation of the framework for typestate mining, as well as an evaluation of how useful enriched specifications are for a real-world application.

TAUTOKO uses techniques from several different areas of software engineering. The following sections summarize related work in the fields of test case generation, typestate verification, and specification mining.

7.5.1 Test Case Generation

There is a large body of work on test case generation, which is why we will limit the discussion to only a few representative approaches. If available, we cite surveys that provide more details in specific areas.

Several approaches use simple *randomized* algorithms to generate tests. Ciupa et al. [21] apply random testing to several industrial sized applications. Their work uses the AUTOTEST approach, which relies on invariants as test oracles. Milicevic et al. [77] present KORAT, which also leverages preconditions but works for JAVA programs. In contrast to random techniques, TAUTOKO specifically generates test cases to enrich a given initial model.

Another area in test case generation are *search-based* techniques. The majority of these approaches systematically analyze control-flow. Symbolic execution [60] simulates execution of the program using symbolic values rather than concrete ones and relies on constraint solvers to derive test data. Recently (e.g. [72]), combinations of concrete and symbolic execution were proposed to overcome limitations of symbolic execution in terms of scalability. A survey of existing search-based approaches can be found in [73]. In contrast to these approaches, TAUTOKO mutates the program to explore new behavior, thus changing the control flow rather than analyzing it.

TAUTOKO is an instance of a *model-based* test generation tool. Such tools require the presence of a model that describes the intended system behavior. This model is then used to derive tests or input data. They come in very different forms, e.g. as finite state machines, or algebraic specifications. A survey on existing model-based approaches can be found in [53]. One example of a model-based testing tool is SPECEXPLORER [104], which is developed by Microsoft Research. SPECEXPLORER explores specifications written in SPEC# [8] model-checking techniques and provides test cases for explored behavior.

The idea of mutating the test suite to generate test cases was inspired by work of Tonella et al. [103]. They propose *evolutionary testing:* using genetic algorithms, an initially generated test suite is mutated to satisfy a given coverage criterion. In contrast to evolutionary testing, TAUTOKO uses a model to guide test case generation. To our knowledge, we are the first that use test generation techniques to improve the quality of mined specifications.

In the area of web application testing, Mesbah et al. [74] extract state machines that describe the user interface of AJAX applications. Their tool called ATUSA derives sequences of operations that are executed to explore the application and trigger bugs. In contrast, our approach explores JAVA classes and generates new tests to enrich specifications.

Gupta and Heidepriem [50] explore a new structural coverage criterion based on dynamic invariants. They use DAIKON [39] to mine an initial set of likely invariants. Based on this set, Gupta and Heidepriem generate a new test suite that tries to cover as many invariants as possible. This test suite can be used to remove spurious invariants from the initial set. In contrast, TAUTOKO mines typestate automata and uses mutation to generate new tests.

7.5.2 Typestate Verification

The term typestate was introduced in 1986 by Strom et al. [99]. Initially, typestates were used to distinguish uninitialized and valid pointers. This information was used to detect potential null pointer dereferences and memory leaks in PASCAL programs.

Since then, several approaches have been developed for different platforms such as .NET [32] or JAVA [46] with varying levels of precision. A promising sound typestate verifier for JAVA was presented by Fink et al. [40]. The tool uses a staged approach with a total of four stages: early stages use imprecise and fast techniques to filter instances that need not be considered in later (more precise and thus expensive) stages. The last stage is only required for objects referenced by more than one method or objects stored in collections. Fink et al. report analysis times ranging from one to ten minutes for projects with up to 200 classes. In contrast to their approach, JFTA is less precise due to its lack of flow-sensitivity. We would expect that using the tool by Fink et al. would further reduce the number of false positives in our evaluation.

7.5.3 Specification Mining

The large body of work on mining specifications can be grouped into dynamic and static approaches. The first technique by Cook and Wolf [23] considers the general problem of extracting a finite state machine based model from an event trace. They reduce the problem to the well-known grammar inference problem [48] and discuss algorithmic, statistical and hybrid approaches. Later, Larus et al. [1] proposed mining specifications for automatic verification. Their approach learns probabilistic finite state automata for C programs. Following the assumption that common behavior is correct behavior, Larus et al. use the inferred automata to search for anomalies in other executions of the program.

Among the first approaches that specifically mine models for classes is the work by Whaley et al. [108]. Their technique mines models with anonymous states and slices models by grouping methods that access the same fields. Lorenzoli et al. [70] mine so-called extended finite state machines with anonymous states. To compress models, the gk-tail algorithm merges states that have the same k-future.

In terms of static techniques, there is also a huge number of different approaches. Wasylkowski et al. [105] mine object usage models that describe the usage of an object in a program. They apply concept analysis to find code locations where rules derived from usage models are violated. Ramanathan et al. [85] use an inter-procedural path-sensitive analysis to infer preconditions for method invocations. Shoham et al. [94] discover that static mining of automata based specifications requires precise aliasing information to produce reliable results.

In the area of web services, Bertolino et al. [9] mine behavior protocols that describe the usage of a web service. The approach uses a sequence of synthesis and testing stages that uses heuristics to refine an initially mined automaton. In contrast, TAUTOKO mines typestate automata for JAVA programs.

7.6 Conclusions

Dynamic specification mining is a promising technique, but its effectiveness entirely depends on the observed executions. If not enough tests are available, the resulting specification may be too incomplete to be useful. By systematically generating test cases, our TAUTOKO prototype explores previously unobserved aspects of the execution space. The resulting enriched specifications cover more general behavior and much more exceptional behavior.

An evaluation with six different subjects shows that TAUTOKO is able to enrich specifications with new transitions in all cases. With enriched specifications, a typestate verifier produces significantly more true positives, and significantly fewer false positives. Generally, we expect test case generation to be applicable to all techniques of dynamic specification mining, generally improving the effectiveness of mined specifications.

Our initial motivation for starting this work was to help developers avoid misusing third party libraries. With the help of TAUTOKO, we can now mine useful specifications for such libraries. To further support developers, we have built an integration of our typestate verifier into ECLIPSE. If the plugin is turned on, ECLIPSE will trigger the typestate verifier whenever a user saves a new version of his project. If the verifier detects a violation, it will mark the appropriate location in the source code as shown in Figure 7.6.

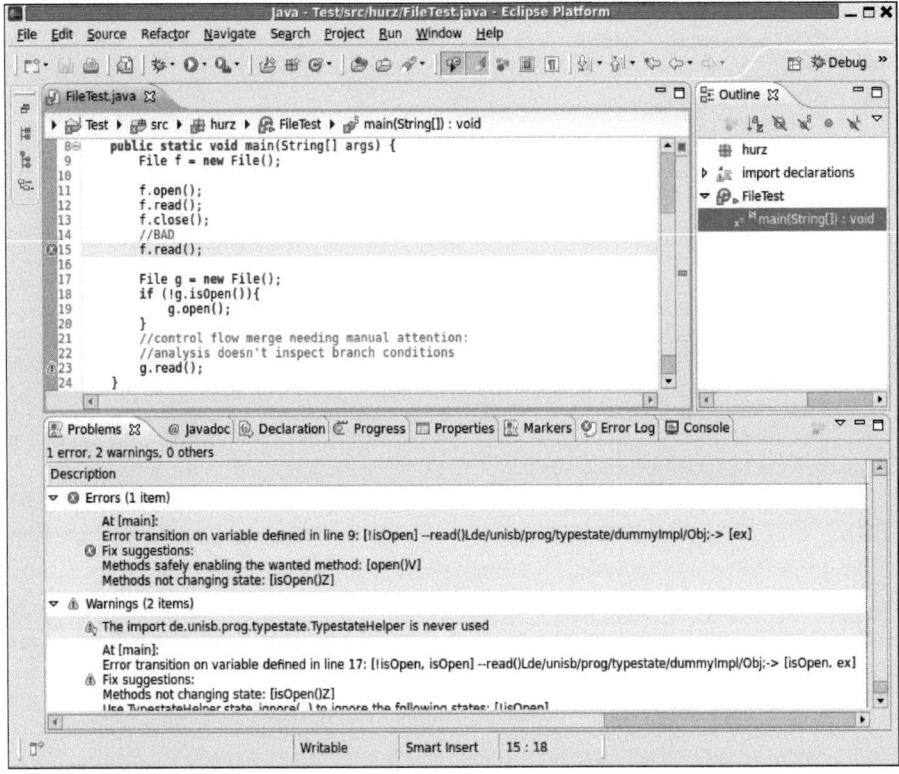

Figure 7.6: A screenshot of the ECLIPSE integration for JFTA.

Chapter 8

Generating Fixes from Object Behavior Anomalies

Recent years have seen considerable advances in automated debugging: sophisticated program analysis guides the programmer along dependencies [63], statistical debugging highlights execution features that correlate with failures [57, 67, 36], and experimental techniques automatically isolate failure causes in the input [120] or program changes [22]. All these techniques narrow down the set of possible bug locations, presenting the programmer with a list of likely locations.

Even with automated bug localization, the programmer must still assess these locations to choose where and how to fix the program. The goal of the work presented in this chapter is to automate this final step as well, effectively automating the entire debugging process for a significant subset of programming errors.

The following example, simple but addressing a real-life application illustrates the approach. The APACHE MINA project provides a framework for building network applications. The project's bug database contains an entry for bug 293, complaining that test `VmPipeBindTest` crashes with an assertion error. To debug the failure, we first want to know how the failing run differs from passing runs; we are searching for *anomalies* that correlate with the failure.

Our approach to finding anomalies is to compare object behavior models from passing and failing runs. Figure 8.1 shows a combined model for the MINA `BaseIo- Acceptor` class; the solid transitions occur in the passing runs. In the passing run, clients call `setLocalAddress()`, then `setHandler()` to set up the attributes; a sequence of alternating `bind()` and `unbind()` calls then alters the object state.

The failing run follows different transitions, shown by dashed lines in the figure. Besides a different method call order when setting up the object, the client now calls `unbind()` multiple times in a row—even when the `bound` attribute is already false. This behavior occurs only in the failing run. But is it also the cause of the failure? To investigate this, we *systematically generate patches* based on differences in models mined from passing and failing runs. The generated patches alter the failing run to match the behavior from the passing runs. If a patch fixes the failure and does not break the regression test suite, we consider it valid.

In the example, there are several ways to change the behavior from failing to passing: we can

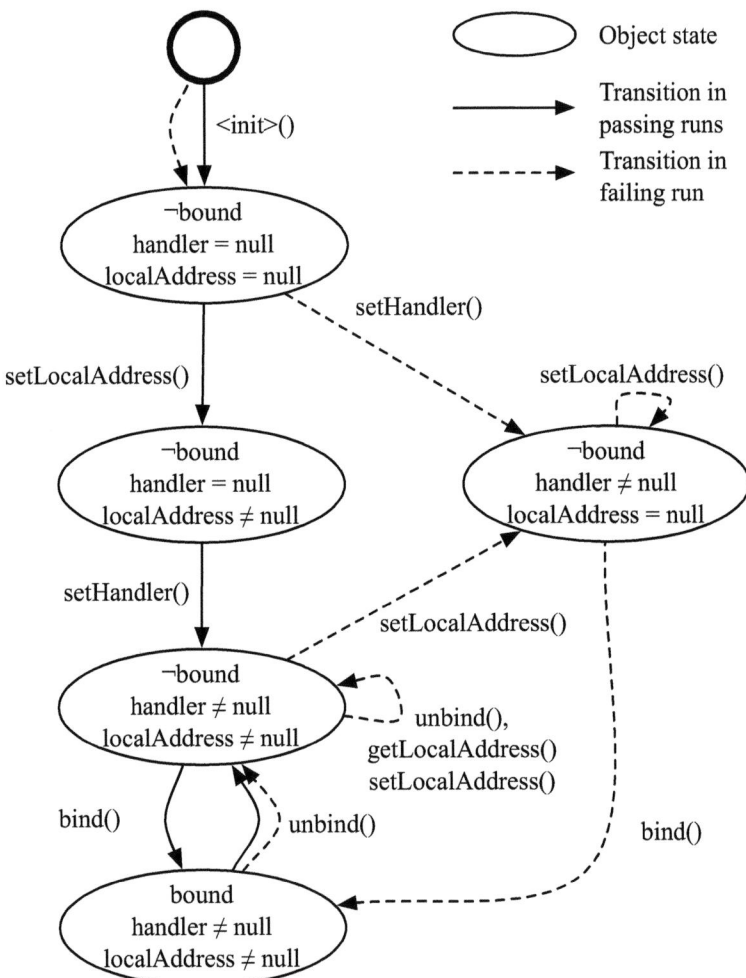

Figure 8.1: A combined model of passing and failing runs for the MINA `BaseIoAcceptor` class. In the failing run, `unbind()` is invoked when the acceptor is not bound.

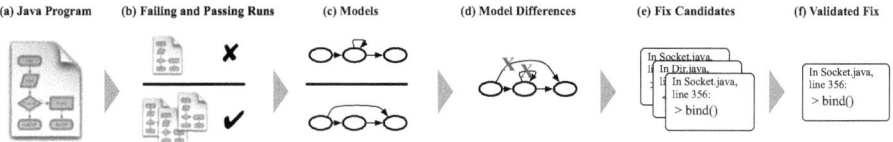

Figure 8.2: How PACHIKA works. PACHIKA takes a JAVA program (a) and out of its passing and failing runs (b), it mines object behavior models (c). From differences (d) between the models, it derives fix candidates (e), which it then validates against automated quality assurance (e.g., a regression test suite). Only validated fixes remain (f).

(a) make the call to `unbind()` conditional such that it only occurs when `bound` is true (as in the passing run), or (b) insert a `bind()` call to reach the correct state in which `unbind()` can be called. All of these *fix candidates* would be valid at this level of abstraction—but would they also work for the concrete program?

We have built a tool called PACHIKA[1] that extracts the above models from passing and failing runs of programs (currently in JAVA), compares the models to determine anomalies, and automatically generates possible fixes. PACHIKA validates the fixes against the original failing run, ensuring that the fix indeed solves the problem at hand; it also runs the program's regression test suite to minimize the risk of introducing new problems. Only fixes that pass this validation will eventually be presented to the programmer.

In the MINA example, PACHIKA finds that the fix candidate (a) introduces an alternate failure in the failing run, while candidate (b)—inserting an additional `bind()` call—passes all the tests; this candidate is the fix PACHIKA suggests to the programmer. Incidentally, this is also how the real MINA bug was eventually fixed as indicated by the project's history.

The rest of this chapter presents the details of the above approach, and we evaluate its performance on real-life programs with real-life bugs. We make the following contributions:

- We present a technique to automatically *derive fix candidates* from anomalies in program executions (Section 8.3). To our knowledge, this is the first time that fixes are directly generated from mined specifications.

- We present a method for *validating these fix candidates* using the failing run as well as automated quality assurance (Section 8.4), eventually suggesting the best fix.

- We evaluate the *effectiveness and the efficiency of the approach* on the IBUGS collection of real-life bugs (Section 8.5).

The remainder of this chapter is organized along the individual stages of PACHIKA (Figure 8.2). In the first step, PACHIKA uses the tracer of ADABU (Section 5.1) to trace the execution of a failing and one or more passing runs. After that, the tool analyzes the traces to identify relevant objects and uses ADABU to mine models for these objects (Section 8.1). The tool then searches the models

---
[1] "Pachika" is the Swahili word for "fix", "insert".

from the failing run and identifies method invocations that violate preconditions as specified by the models of the passing run (Section 8.2). PACHIKA then derives fix candidates from model differences (Section 8.3). These fix candidates are validated against the test suite to find the best fix (Section 8.4). Throughout these sections, we will use the MINA example as well as another real-life example taken from the APACHE JDO project to illustrate our approach.

After evaluating effectiveness and efficiency of PACHIKA (Section 8.5), we discuss the general applicability to real-life bugs (Section 8.6). We close with related work (Section 8.7), and conclusion and consequences (Section 8.8).

Parts of this chapter were published at the Automated Software Engineering Conference 2009 [30].

8.1 Mining Models

PACHIKA uses ADABU (Chapter 5) to mine models from passing and failing runs. For the experiments in this chapter, we use the default abstraction function as defined in Section 4.7. In Section 8.1, we introduced another parameter for model mining called model depth. This parameter specifies the number of indirections on the heap ADABU follows when extracting the state of objects. Obviously, increasing the depth of models yields more detailed models. In the context of PACHIKA, an increase in model depth leads to more deviations being flagged, and thus more fix candidates being generated.

For the MINA example, a model depth of one is actually sufficient to generate a good fix for the bug: PACHIKA detects an incorrect value of bound and synthesizes a fix from the passing model. In another real-life example taken from the bug database of the APACHE JDO project, it is necessary to use a model depth of two. In this example, a PersistenceManager class manages objects stored in a database. Internally, PersistenceManager uses a Transaction object to synchronize access to the database. The Transaction object is available to clients via a getter method. For consistency reasons, access to persistent objects requires an active Transaction. In the failing run, a client requests an object by calling getObjectById() when the Transaction is inactive. In all passing runs, this is handled correctly.

Figure 8.3 shows a simplified version[2] of the models for PersistenceManager. The state encompasses the transaction tx, as well as the Transaction object's active flag if the Transaction is not null. Transitions in the state of the PersistenceManager now also occur if a method changes the state of the Transaction. This model captures the interplay between calls to methods getObjectById(), tx.begin() and tx.commit(), which essentially is a protocol that involves two objects. With model depth two, PACHIKA is able to capture this protocol as it includes the state of the Transaction into the state of the PersistenceManager.

To study the effect of the model depth parameter on the results of PACHIKA, we repeat our experiments with model depth one and two.

---

[2]The actual models mined for this example are too large to present here but can be viewed at the project's web page (Section 8.8).

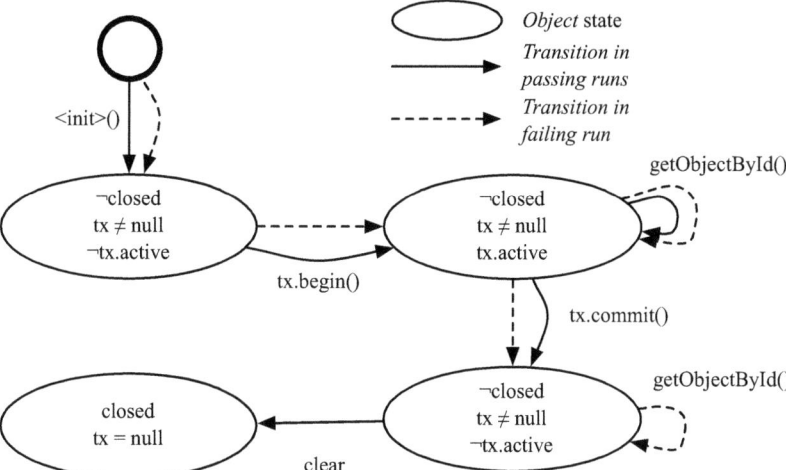

Figure 8.3: A deep model of `PersistenceManager` for the passing and failing runs of bug JDO 28. In the failing run, the second invocation of `getObjectById()` violates the precondition that `tx.active` is `true`.

8.1.1 Mining Preconditions

Every method has a (potentially empty) set of preconditions that need to be satisfied in order to invoke the method successfully. For example, the `unbind()` method in the MINA example has the precondition that `bound` needs to be `true`. To find anomalies, PACHIKA mines such preconditions from passing run models and looks for transitions in failing run models that violate these preconditions. In some languages, such as Eiffel, Spec# and JML, programmers would be able to provide preconditions explicitly. In this chapter we are working with plain JAVA programs where preconditions have to be inferred. Section 10 discusses this idea further.

A first approach to mining preconditions from models would be to search for common properties of attributes in states in which a method is invoked. This approach has two disadvantages. First, it limits preconditions to the state of the object the method is invoked on. Second, a method typically does not read all attributes of the state; PACHIKA would thus generate spurious preconditions.

To solve these problems, PACHIKA traces *the set of fields that are read by a method invocation* and generates preconditions only for those fields. For example, in the case of `unbind()`, PACHIKA detects that the method only reads fields `bound` and `handler`, and therefore only looks for preconditions that affect those two fields. If a method reads a field that is part of a parameter, the field will also be included in the set and thus PACHIKA also detects preconditions for fields of parameters.

In practice, identifying the set of relevant fields is more complex than only tracing field reads for every method invocation:

- Many methods create and use *temporary objects*. Field reads on such objects cannot yield preconditions since those objects did not exist when the method was invoked. We therefore only include field reads on objects that existed prior to the invocation.

- Many programs make extensive use of *getter and setter methods*. To retrieve the value of a field, a method invokes a getter rather than accessing the field directly. To deal with this, PACHIKA propagates a field access to the calling method if the accessed object is also visible in the caller.

When generating models, PACHIKA annotates each method invocation in the model with the set of fields read. This information is then used in the next step to detect violations.

8.2 Detecting Violations

The basic technique for detecting anomalies is to compare models of passing and failing runs. From the passing models, PACHIKA learns preconditions for a method invocation and checks the failing model for violations of these preconditions.

Even a very short run of an object-oriented program creates a large number of objects. In MINA, for example, the failing run lasts only 0.3 seconds but generates over 18 000 objects. Analysing all these models, while possible in principle, would take too much time in practice. We need to find a heuristic that reduces the search space by only considering a subset of all objects. A good heuristic selects all objects whose behavior is relevant for the failure, and only few objects that are irrelevant.

One way to approach this is to identify suspicious points in the execution of the program and include all objects that are accessible at those points. The challenge is how to identify such suspicious program points. Depending on the type of the bug at hand, PACHIKA follows two different strategies:

Crashing Bugs For crashing bugs (i.e. bugs that terminate with an exception), our approach includes all objects accessible from methods that were active when the program crashed. The assumption behind this approach is that for crashing bugs, the failure typically occurs close to the infection of the program state. This assumption does not hold for all bugs. In our experience, however, many crashing bugs are fixed in one of the methods that are active when the program crashes. We therefore believe that this heuristic will include the relevant objects in the majority of cases.

Non-crashing Bugs If the program does not crash, but simply produces incorrect output, locating suspicious program points is more difficult. In the current version, PACHIKA uses a JAVA implementation of the TARANTULA [57] fault localization approach to automatically identify suspicious methods. In essence, TARANTULA ranks source code lines based on deviations in the coverage of passing and failing runs. The ranking method puts those lines that were executed often in failing, but seldom or never in passing runs to the top. PACHIKA leverages this ranking to sort all methods executed in the failing run by the maximum rank of all lines in the method. It then investigates a configurable percentage of the highest ranked methods, and looks for anomalies in objects accessible when one of these methods is active.

For each suspicious method, PACHIKA extracts models for all objects that are reachable through the parameters of the methods on the stack. This approach was inspired by work of Artzi et al. [4],

8.2. DETECTING VIOLATIONS

who use a similar technique to reproduce crashes. Unlike that approach, however, PACHIKA does not include all transitively reachable objects, but only follows references up to a certain depth (see Section 8.1).

Once PACHIKA has mined models for all relevant objects from the failing run, the next problem is to choose passing models against which to compare the failing models. PACHIKA currently takes the following approach:

- First, PACHIKA searches the passing run for invocations of the same methods as for the failing run. For every such invocation, PACHIKA extracts objects accessible from the method and compares models for objects that were accessible through the same path in the passing and failing runs. For example, if a method *m* has a first parameter that is of complex type, PACHIKA compares passing and failing models for the first parameter.

- If no method invocation is found in the passing run, PACHIKA identifies the set of classes for which models were mined from the failing run. It then extracts models for all instances of those classes from the passing run and then compares models for the corresponding classes.

- If there are no suitable models in the failing run, PACHIKA is unable to detect any violations and therefore exits without generating a fix.

If PACHIKA is able to find comparable models, it will search the models of the passing run for preconditions of method invocations. For every method *m* that is part of the model, PACHIKA examines all invocations of *m* and extracts the values for all fields accessed by *m* (see Section 8.1.1). PACHIKA then mines the values for each field and tries to derive simple preconditions such as a field having the same value before all invocations of a method. The tool currently has its own engine to detect preconditions. If necessary, however, it could use DAIKON's [39] invariant detection engine to mine more complex preconditions.

The final step for detecting violations is to check all method invocations from the failing model to see whether they violate any of the preconditions mined from the passing model. If a method invocation violates at least one precondition, PACHIKA remembers the violated preconditions, as well as the state in which the violating method was invoked.

For the MINA example, PACHIKA finds three relevant objects. The passing run does not include an invocation of the crashing method, and therefore PACHIKA compares models based on classes. PACHIKA only finds one model with violations, shown in Figure 8.1. The violation is that unbind() in the passing run is only being called when bound is true. Note that PACHIKA does not extract preconditions for setLocalAddress() and setHandler(), as those methods do not read fields.

For the JDO example, PACHIKA mines three models from the failing run and compares them based on their classes. Altogether, there are 4 violations, one of which is that getObjectById() requires tx.active to be true.

8.3 Generating Fixes

For each invocation of a method *m* that violates at least one precondition, PACHIKA generates fix candidates based on the passing and failing models. In general, there are two possibilities to fix a violation based on models. The first is to satisfy the preconditions of *m* by *inserting calls* that make the necessary changes to the state. The second strategy is to avoid the violation by *deleting the violating call to m*[3].

8.3.1 Inserting Calls

In order to satisfy the preconditions of a method *m*, PACHIKA searches the failing and passing models for states that satisfy the preconditions and searches for a path to any of them. For example, the violating method call in MINA happens in a state where bound is false. The precondition from the passing run requires bound to be true. PACHIKA finds one state that satisfies this condition and two possible paths from the violating state to the correct state:

1. The first path is to invoke setLocalAddress() first and then bind(). This path is not considered because setLocal Address() requires an argument, and PACHIKA cannot synthesize arguments.[4]

2. The second path is to invoke only bind(). This is a fix candidate as produced by PACHIKA.

Every feasible path is translated into code which injects calls to all methods on the path right before the violating method call.

8.3.2 Deleting Calls

The second strategy is to avoid the violation by deleting the method call if at least one precondition is violated. Depending on where the fix is to be applied, we can remove the call at either the caller or the callee site. To remove callee invocations, PACHIKA generates an if-block that checks the precondition at the beginning of the method, and adds a return instruction as the content of the if-block. At the caller site, PACHIKA also creates an if-block that suppresses the call if the precondition is violated. If the removed method has a return type other than void, we try default values such as true, false or null.

For MINA, PACHIKA generates a fix candidate consisting of an if-block around the method call to unbind() such that the method is only invoked if bound is true.

---

[3] In Chapter 7, we use similar techniques to explore new edges in a model.
[4] Generally, PACHIKA is limited to methods that do not take arguments. We are aware that this is a severe restriction. However, synthesizing arguments for method invocations is a problem in itself and is therefore left for future work.

8.4 Choosing the Best Fix

We refer to the non-validated fixes generated by PACHIKA as the set of *fix candidates*. Each fix candidate is applied in isolation and evaluated in two steps. First, we execute the failing test. If the fix changes the outcome to passing, we call it a *potential fix*. For each potential fix, we subject it to the program's automated quality assurance—in our case, all tests of the program's regression test suite. If the fix does not alter the outcome of any one test, we refer to it as a *validated fix*. Only validated fixes will be presented to the programmer as proposed fixes for the failure.

In the case of MINA, PACHIKA generates two candidate fixes, out of which one is successfully validated against the test suite. The fix is to add a call to `bind()` which ensures that the precondition for `unbind()` is satisfied. For JDO, PACHIKA generates 8 fix candidates, of which only one is a potential fix that is validated successfully against the test suite. The fix is to insert a call to `tx.begin()` right before the second call to `getObjectById()`.

Both fixes are semantically equivalent to the fixes that were applied by the developers, and thus can be considered to be valid fixes for the failures.

The notion of "best fix" raises the question whether PACHIKA can produce "bad" fixes, too. If a suggested fix passes all tests but is considered incorrect, the test suite should be improved—very much like, in mutation testing [33], an undetected mutation implies a weakness in the test suite. As soon as the test suite (or generally, automated quality assurance) is set up to catch the invalid fix, PACHIKA will filter it out.

8.5 Experimental Evaluation

In the previous sections, we have seen how PACHIKA was able to generate successful fixes for two bugs as they occurred in real-life. The two examples were found by analyzing the bug databases of MINA and JDO, manually inspecting the bug reports, extracting the faulty version from the source repository, building and running the test suites. This is a lot of manual effort and is not feasible for a larger study.

To evaluate the effectiveness of our approach, we ran PACHIKA on the two subjects provided by the IBUGS repository [31]. IBUGS contains programs together with test runs and bugs as they actually occurred in the history of the project. For a subset of the bugs, IBUGS also provides test cases that reproduce the problem, which we refer to as failing tests. In our experiments, we use the projects' regression test suites as passing runs.

8.5.1 Subjects

Table 8.1 summarizes information about the subjects used in the IBUGS study. Column "Crashing Bugs" gives the number of bugs that caused the program to crash. We included all these bugs in our study. For each bug in the repository, IBUGS contains a snapshot of the project right before and right after the bug was fixed. Thus, the size of the project and the number of tests varies from bug to bug.

Program	Crashing Bugs	Size (LOC)	Number of Tests
MINA	1	14,773	89
JDO	1	64,017	437
ASPECTJ	18	75,123	1,178
RHINO	8	37,902	1,499

Table 8.1: Subjects used in the evaluation. The first two rows show characteristics of the examples used. The last two rows give details on the subjects used in the evaluation. Size was measured using David A. Wheeler's *sloccount*.

Columns "Size" and "Number of Tests" therefore list only the values for the latest bug included in the study.

8.5.2 Experimental Setup

Currently, PACHIKA requires only one configuration parameter: the model depth used when mining models with ADABU (cf. Section 8.1). As explained above, the model depth influences the set of bugs PACHIKA is able to detect. To study the impact of increasing model depth, we ran PACHIKA twice, once with model depth one and once with model depth two. In our experience, increasing the model depth beyond two generates models that are too detailed to be useful. Also, the time required to run the experiments increases significantly for model depth values beyond two. Thus, a maximum depth of two is a reasonable compromise between speed and the range of violations that PACHIKA can detect and possibly fix. The general problem of choosing the right depth is further discussed in Section 8.5.6.

8.5.3 Running the Experiments

To conduct the experiments, we perform the following steps:

1. First, we collect all bugs in the repository for which there is at least one test case that reproduces the failure and group them into crashing and non-crashing bugs. This yields 18 crashing and 16 non-crashing bugs for ASPECTJ, as well as 12 crashing and 7 non-crashing bugs for RHINO.

2. PACHIKA traces the failing run and identifies the set of interesting objects. The approach used to identify interesting objects depends on the type of the bug (crashing vs. non-crashing, see Section 8.2). For each such object, a model is mined from the failing run. The remaining steps are performed for each passing test in the test suite.

3. PACHIKA traces the passing run and searches the trace for executions of the crashing method. If at least one invocation is found, models for all visible objects are mined just like for the failing run. If no invocation is found, PACHIKA mines models for all classes for which at least one model was extracted from the failing run (cf. Section 8.2).

	Tracing Overhead	Trace File Size	Model Mining
Subject	(factor)	(MB)	(s)
MINA	29	42	34
JDO	16	356	212
ASPECTJ	9	223	110
RHINO	26	11	8

Table 8.2: Tracing overhead and execution times for all subjects.

4. If the previous step yields at least one model, PACHIKA compares models to generate candidate fixes for all active methods as described in Section 8.3. Each candidate fix is first checked against the failing test and then against the test suite (cf. Section 8.4).

8.5.4 Performance

Our experiments were performed on a 2 GHz AMD machine with a maximum of 2 Gigabytes of memory. Table 8.2 lists information about overhead and execution times. For MINA and JDO, results are averages over all runs in the test suite. For ASPECTJ and RHINO, we give averages for the latest version used in the experiments. Tracing overhead is expressed as the factor by which execution time increases when tracing is turned on. The third column gives the execution time the model miner takes to extract models for depth one (cf. Section 8.1).

Table 8.2 does not list times PACHIKA takes to generate fixes, since they are negligible compared to the other steps. The time needed to validate a candidate fix is equivalent to the execution time of the test suite for almost all candidates. In some cases, a fix candidate causes the program to loop endlessly. In that case, we terminate the run after a timeout of two minutes and consider the test as failed.

As is to be expected, tracing incurs a huge amount of runtime overhead. Since both ASPECTJ and RHINO contain over 1000 tests, tracing and mining the test suite was the most time-consuming part in our experiments. For example, tracing and mining all 1038 runs in the test suite of bug #87376 takes a little less than two days. Unfortunately this needs to be done for each investigated bug, since each bug is fixed in a different version of the code base.

In practice, however, tracing and mining the test suite only needs to happen once for each released version of a program. As soon as a new version is released to the public, we can trace the test suite, mine models for all objects in the traces, and store them for reuse. For every bug report filed for the new version, we can reuse the cached models.

8.5.5 Results

The results for crashing and non-crashing bugs of ASPECTJ are summarized in Tables 8.3 and 8.4. Table 8.5 lists results for all bugs in RHINO. For each investigated bug, we give the number of candidate, potential, and validated fixes (cf. Section 8.4) for model depth one (columns two to five)

| | Depth 1 | | | | Depth 2 | | | |
| | Candidates | | Fixes | | Candidates | | Fixes | |
Bug	Insert	Delete	Potential	Validated	Insert	Delete	Potential	Validated
#34925	0	0	0	0	20	32	0	0
#36803	1	0	0	0	81	79	26	0
#39993	0	6	0	0	113	51	0	0
#43033	0	0	0	0	28	12	0	0
#51320	0	0	0	0	0	0	0	0
#51322	13	1	0	0	71	42	43	1
#62642	68	0	0	0	753	23	0	0
#64331	2	1	0	0	69	5	0	0
#65319	3	2	0	0	161	4	0	0
#67774	41	6	0	0	359	14	2	0
#68991	68	0	0	0	946	23	0	0
#70619	0	0	0	0	26	0	0	0
#71377	68	0	0	0	946	23	0	0
#72528	68	0	0	0	979	19	0	0
#80249	68	0	0	0	766	26	0	0
#87376	2	6	0	0	19	43	0	0
#121616	128	0	38	1	183	0	45	1
#173602	3	0	1	1	459	13	147	15

Table 8.3: Results of the experimental evaluation for crashing bugs in ASPECTJ with model depth one and two.

and two (columns six to nine).

For ASPECTJ, PACHIKA generates fix candidates for 31 out of 34 bugs. For a total of nine bugs, there is at least one potential fix, out of which four are successfully validated against the test suite. For RHINO, PACHIKA is able to generate fixes for 15 out of 19 bugs, of which seven have at least one fix candidate. A validated fix is found for only one bug. In the next sections, we take a closer look at all cases in which PACHIKA is able to generate a validated fix. After that, we compare our results for different subjects and model depth values, as well as crashing vs. non-crashing bugs.

Checking for a null reference

Bug #173602 in ASPECTJ manifests itself as a NullPointerException in method resolve() in class InterTypeMethodDeclaration. PACHIKA detects one violation for the invocation of resolve(), namely that binding must not be null. The *delete method call* strategy generates the fix as shown in Figure 8.4. The actual fix applied by the developers also amounts to a conditional

| | Depth 1 | | | | Depth 2 | | | |
| | Candidates | | Fixes | | Candidates | | Fixes | |
Bug	Insert	Delete	Potential	Validated	Insert	Delete	Potential	Validated
#37739	95	15	11	0	1921	189	86	0
#42993	139	35	0	0	1831	165	112	0
#47754	129	8	0	0	1366	118	0	0
#49457	8	0	0	0	164	5	0	0
#49638	89	18	0	0	2214	640	0	0
#53981	43	4	0	0	1040	68	0	0
#53999	47	5	0	0	504	249	0	0
#54421	361	9	0	0	2772	150	0	0
#55341	123	43	4	0	1198	316	67	0
#60015	44	30	0	0	**746**	**1090**	**215**	**130**
#61536	10	5	0	0	468	23	0	0
#64069	80	7	0	0	1198	266	0	0
#69459	60	2	0	0	1115	79	0	0
#72157	27	3	0	0	981	50	0	0
#72531	0	0	0	0	0	0	0	0
#76096	0	0	0	0	0	0	0	0

Table 8.4: Results of the experimental evaluation for non-crashing bugs in ASPECTJ with model depth one and two.

| | Depth One | | | | Depth Two | | | |
| | Candidates | | Fixes | | Candidates | | Fixes | |
Bug	Insert	Delete	Potential	Validated	Insert	Delete	Potential	Validated
#114491	0	650	0	0	13	2	0	0
#114493	982	1	0	0	6930	1	0	0
#159334	0	0	0	0	161	5	0	0
#179068	0	60	0	0	297	68	0	0
#191668	0	0	0	0	0	15	0	0
#191688	0	0	0	0	0	0	0	0
#194364	1273	16	0	0	17941	105	0	0
#193555	12	78	0	0	98	155	0	0
#203402	0	0	0	0	0	0	0	0
#203841	0	0	0	0	0	0	0	0
#220584	335	11	1	0	721	7	0	0
#210682	1300	946	2	0	1628	1128	3	0
#137181	1999	184	22	0	7507	16	0	0
#157509	0	0	0	0	**292**	**39**	**33**	**16**
#177314	10	1	0	0	0	0	0	0
#181654	1659	488	9	0	33	0	0	0
#181834	3672	163	181	0	27090	108	1424	0
#184107	3	78	0	0	1066	1400	35	0
#185165	0	0	0	0	1	0	0	0

Table 8.5: Results of the experimental evaluation for all bugs in RHINO with model depth one and two. Crashing bugs are listed in the first part of the table, while the lower part shows results fro non-crashing bugs.

8.5. EXPERIMENTAL EVALUATION

```
  public void resolve(ClassScope upperScope) {
>       // Fix from source repository
>       if (binding == null) ignoreFurtherInvestigation = true;
>       // Fix generated by PACHIKA
>       if (binding == null) {
>           return;
>       }
      if (munger == null) ignoreFurtherInvestigation = true;
      if (ignoreFurtherInvestigation) return;
          ...
      }
  }
```

Figure 8.4: The proposed fix for bug #173602 is to not execute method `resolve()` if the precondition for `binding` is violated.

```
  public boolean visit(MethodDeclaration methodDeclaration,
                       ClassScope scope) {
>     // Fix generated by PACHIKA
>     // is the same as in the source repository
>     if (methodDeclaration.hasErrors()) {
>         return false;
>     }
      ContextToken tok = CompilationAndWeavingContext.
             enteringPhase(...);
          ...
  }
```

Figure 8.5: The fix for bug #121616 suppresses the violation by aborting the execution in case `methodDeclaration` has errors.

return which additionally sets the `ignoreFurtherInvestigation` flag. This flag is later used by ASPECTJ to stop processing the declaration object. However, not setting the flag in this situation does not cause any problems, since none of the tests in the test suite later fails.

Checking for error conditions

In the failing run of bug #121616, a `NullPointerException` is raised in `buildFormal-AdviceBindingsFrom()` of class `ValidateAtAspectJAnnotationsVisitor`. When comparing failing and passing run models, PACHIKA detects a precondition violation for parameter `methodDeclaration`, namely that the `ignoreFurtherInvestigation` flag which is returned by `hasErrors()` is `true`. The delete method strategy generates a conditional return in case that this precondition is violated (Figure 8.5). In this case, the generated fix is equal to the fix applied by the developers.

Invoking methods to set default state

The failing run for bug #51322 crashes ASPECTJ by causing a `NullPointerEx- ception` in method `build()` of class `InterTypeMethodDeclaration`. Figure 8.6 shows the relevant parts of this method, together with the fix as applied by the developers, and the fix generated by

```
  public EclipseTypeMunger build(ClassScope classScope) {
    ...
    if(ignoreFurtherInvestigation) { return null;
    } else {
      binding = classScope.referenceContext.
                  binding.resolveTypesFor(binding);
>     // Fix generated by PACHIKA
>     binding.constantPoolDeclaringClass().
>         addDefaultAbstractMethods();
>     binding.constantPoolDeclaringClass().methods();
>     // Fix from source repository
>     if (binding == null) {
>       throw new AbortCompilation();
>     }
      ResolvedMember sig = new ResolvedMember(...);
        ...
    }
  }
```

Figure 8.6: The proposed fix for bug #51322 invokes methods that initialize values, essentially avoiding the illegal access in a subsequent invocation of build().

PACHIKA. The failing run contains two invocations of method build(), of which only the last one fails. For the first invocation, PACHIKA detects a precondition violation for the declaringClass attribute in the binding variable. The model from the passing run contains a path that repairs this violation, which consists of invoking addDefaultAbstractMethods() and methods(). When this fix is applied to ASPECTJ, the state of binding is altered such that the second invocation of build() no longer occurs and the failing run passes. The fixed version also passes all the other tests.

The developer's fix for this problem is simply to abort the execution of build(), which is very different from PACHIKA's fix. However, both fixes comply with the specification as given by the program's test suite.[5]

Unnecessary warnings

Bug #60015 of ASPECTJ is a non-crashing bug concerned with unnecessary warnings the compiler outputs if an input file contains an interface. The actual fix committed by the developers (Figure 8.7) is to recognize these cases and suppress outputting the message.

Since the bug does not raise an exception, PACHIKA uses TARANTULA to find suspicious program points and looks for anomalies in the top 20 methods. A surprisingly large number of 130 validated fixes are generated. Many of these are concerned with the same precondition. The fixes differ in the position within the method where the precondition is checked. We investigated a subset of ten validated fixes[6] and found that eight of them are concerned with code that outputs warnings. The effect of all these patches is that some warnings usually output by ASPECTJ are not printed. It is

---

[5]If Pachika's fix would be considered incorrect, a simple remedy is to extend the test suite appropriately, as discussed in Section 8.4. We asked the developer who committed the original fix for his opinion, but did not get a reply.

[6]Estimating the effect of a patch is very time-consuming, mostly because we are no experts of the system.

8.5. EXPERIMENTAL EVALUATION

```
        private void warnOnConfusingSig(Shadow shadow) {
        // no warnings for declare error/warning
        if (munger instanceof Checker) return;
        ...
>       // Fix committed by developers
>       // PR60015 - Don't report the warning if the declaring type
>       // is object and 'this' is an interface
>       if (exactDeclaringType.isInterface(world) &&
>             shadowDeclaringType.equals(world.resolve("java.lang.Object"))) {
>           return;
>       }
        ...
```

Figure 8.7: For bug #60015, PACHIKA generates several candidates that suppress warnings output by the compiler.

unclear, whether these warnings are actually useful. At the very least, there is no test case in the whole test suite of ASPECTJ that ever tests for any of these messages.

Incorrect escaping

The symptom for bug #157509 of RHINO is that illegal identifiers with escapes are not rejected. Instead, RHINO processes them and outputs an incorrect value. The fixing change applied by the developers churns a total of 310 lines, of which 195 are actually relevant to fix the problem (see Section 6.5.2 on page 81). In essence, this fix recognizes escaped characters in identifiers and treats them correctly. This is a non-crashing bug, and therefore PACHIKA runs TARANTULA to find suspicious methods. In total PACHIKA generates 16 validated fixes, all of which affect method `getToken()` in class `TokenStream`. This method is responsible for parsing the input file. All of the generated patches alter `getToken()` such that a character signaling the end of file is returned, which in turn causes RHINO to exit. Clearly, this is no valid way of fixing the bug. However, similar to the previous bug, none of the tests in the test suite recognizes this problem, which is why PACHIKA considers it to be a valid fix.

8.5.6 Discussion

Model Depth

In our experiments, increasing model depth from one to two causes PACHIKA to generate more fix candidates. For bug #194364 for example, model depth two yields more than ten times as many fix candidates as model depth one. This is not surprising, as an increase in model depth leads to more complex models, and thus to more possibilities to create fixes. Of the five bugs for which PACHIKA generates at least one validated fix, three require a model depth of two. Thus, at least for our experimental setting, running PACHIKA with model depth two yields considerably more validated fixes.

Delete vs. Insert

In most cases where PACHIKA detects a violation, both fix strategies generate fixes. In terms of the numbers of generated fixes, both strategies are also roughly equivalent. In some cases, the *insert method call* strategy generates a large number of fixes due to many different paths through the model. However, the delete strategy generates validated fixes for four bugs, compared to four bugs for the insert strategy. Thus, in our experiments, deleting method calls is more successful when it comes to generating a validated fix.

AspectJ versus Rhino

Our results show that PACHIKA works much better on ASPECTJ than on RHINO. We examined the log files of our experiments and found two possible causes:

- RHINO is considerably smaller than ASPECTJ and contains only a very small number of classes that have complex models (see Section 8.6). Thus, PACHIKA finds only a small number of violations per bug.

- In many cases where a violation is found, technical restrictions such as the limitation to methods without parameters prevent PACHIKA from generating a fix. We hope to remove some of these restrictions in the near future and thus be able to generate more fixes for RHINO.

Inadequate test suites

The validated fixes for bugs #51322, #157509 and #60015 highlight a problem for approaches that validate fixes using the test suite: The quality of validated fixes is highly dependent on the quality of the test suite. A bad test suite will cause many fixes to be validated successfully and thus a lot of false positives to be presented to the user. However, in the absence of a formal specification, a test suite is still the best way to automatically assess the impact of a change on the program.

8.5.7 Threats to Validity

As with any empirical study, the interpretation of the results is subject to several limitations.

External Validity The scope of our study is limited, as it only investigates 53 bugs in two programs. Therefore, the results of our experiments are hardly generalizable. However, it is difficult to conduct a controlled experiment with realistic data since there is only little such data available. A manual investigation, as we did it on MINA and JDO, requires a lot of effort and is also difficult to reproduce for other researchers. Although we are aware of these limitations, we believe that our evaluation is realistic since it uses real post-release bugs[7] and relies only on test runs from a bug database or the test suite.

---
[7]We expect an evaluation of PACHIKA on artificially seeded bugs to yield much better results—in particular if seeding includes addition or deletion of method calls, as most mutation testing approaches do.

Internal Validity PACHIKA is a complex system that consists of almost 30 000 lines of code. We verified the correctness of model mining and fix generation for several small artificial test cases. However, the huge amount of data and the complexity of the system make it impossible to check every step for realistic examples. It may well be that PACHIKA contains errors which cause fixes to be missed or invalid fixes to be generated. However, verifying potential fixes against the test suite ensures that there are no false positives. We encourage other researchers to validate our results. All bugs used in the evaluation are available in the IBUGS dataset. PACHIKA is also available for download; see Chapter 9 for details.

Construct Validity PACHIKA uses the test suite as a source of program runs. As such, it depends on the tests to correctly classify a run as passing or failing. In some cases, this check is not precise enough. For example, some tests in ASPECTJ simply check the output for a certain keyword, which may lead to a test outcome incorrectly being classified as passing. However, we observed this problem only for a small number of tests and are confident that the huge number of tests ensures a high quality of fixes that are presented to the user.

There also is a risk that PACHIKA generates fixes that only apply to the symptom at hand, rather than the problem root cause ("The method crashes when `p` is `null`, so let's insert a check for it"). This risk is best countered by quality assurance; in particular, any increased level of automated validation (such as contracts or widespread program proofs) will automatically filter out more bad fix candidates as generated by PACHIKA. Indeed, our evaluation indicates that this is already the case.

8.6 Applicability

After coming to the conclusion that automatic fixing of failing programs was indeed feasible for some cases, we wanted to investigate the general applicability of tools like PACHIKA. In the experimental evaluation in Section 8.5, our tool was only able to generate fix candidates for a small number of bugs in RHINO, since only few bugs actually revealed violations of preconditions. Obviously, PACHIKA's applicability is limited to bugs that cause a precondition violation. In order to get a feeling of PACHIKA's potential, we wanted to know *how many bugs actually show precondition violations.*

For this purpose, we investigated a sample of bugs from the bug databases of the projects used in the evaluation. For each bug, we tried to determine whether or not the bug would have caused a violation of a precondition. However, we quickly came to the conclusion that it is not possible to reliably answer this question by only looking at the bug report and source code. On the other hand, manually building and executing each snapshot for a large enough set of bugs is too time-consuming.

PACHIKA's ability to detect bugs correlates with the number of classes that may potentially be used in a wrong way. A high percentage of such classes would mean that there is a big potential for wrong usage that causes violations. To measure the percentage, we generated models for all classes used in our subjects and classified models as having preconditions or not. A model has preconditions

	Number of Classes	Classes with preconditions
MINA	166	15
JDO	377	116
ASPECTJ	443	154
RHINO	52	17

Table 8.6: How prevalent are classes with preconditions? With the exception of MINA, roughly one third of all classes are complex enough to be misused.

if there is at least one method invocation other than that of a getter method which requires another method to be invoked before. For example, in Figure 8.1, the model for VmPipeAcceptor has preconditions, because in order to satisfy the precondition of unbind(), method bind() has to be invoked before.

Table 8.6 lists the number of classes for which we mined at least one model (column 2), and the number of classes with preconditions (column 3). Except for MINA, approximately *one out of three classes has a model with preconditions*. Thus, roughly one third of the classes in our projects are complex enough to be misused. Since there are typically several objects with different types in the scope at any point in the program, there is a big potential for detecting anomalies based on violated preconditions.

8.7 Related Work

8.7.1 Locating Bugs

The most frequent work in automated debugging deals with the problem of *bug localization*—that is, relating a failure to possible bug locations. Milestones in that direction include the TARANTULA approach by Jones et al. [57] as well as *statistical debugging* [67] by Liblit et al., who allow the programmer to focus on a small percentage of the code.

Like these approaches, PACHIKA leverages the *difference* between passing and failing executions; rather than suggesting locations, however, it produces *fixes*. By leveraging the test suite (and all other forms of automated validation), PACHIKA can thus successfully weed out invalid candidates, resulting in either a valid fix—or nothing. This "no-false-positives" approach is where our approach greatly differs from existing bug localization techniques. Nonetheless, it can be easily combined with bug localization: When PACHIKA cannot generate a fix, then bug localization may at least suggest a location; or one could use locations as suggested by a bug localization technique as suspicious locations for PACHIKA (cf. Section 8.2).

8.7.2 Repairing Programs

Most related to PACHIKA is the recent work by Weimer et al. [107] on automatic patch generation. Weimer et al. systematically mutate a failing C program by inserting, swapping, and deleting statements. Their approach then uses an extended form of genetic programming to evolve those mutants that pass (1) the (previously failing) test and (2) as many tests as possible from a regression test suite. The approach produces repairs in less than three minutes on average on a set of ten selected bugs.

Our approach is similar to their technique in that it also generates potential fixes and assesses them via a regression test suite. The contribution and potential of their approach over PACHIKA is clearly the wide range of possible mutations, as well as the adaptive approach in generating fixes.

Rather than using adaptive random search, however, PACHIKA starts right away with behavioral differences between passing and failing runs, which keeps the search space narrow. Such a focus is very much needed: It is unknown whether the approach of Weimer et al. scales up to a program like ASPECTJ, with more than 75,000 lines of code and a test suite where *one single run* already takes a minute; it is also unknown how much fine-tuning of parameters is required to quickly find fixes. It is also unclear how the approach of Weimer et al. could integrate bug localization or mined specifications, as PACHIKA does. Last but not least, we evaluate PACHIKA on *all* previously documented crashing bugs of ASPECTJ and RHINO—and thus get an idea of scalability and applicability on real programs and real bugs.

8.7.3 Leveraging Specifications

Weimer developed a method for automatically and soundly patching programs with a given specification [106]. However, as Weimer states in [107], a formal specification is seldom available—which is why PACHIKA mines and leverages behavior models from passing and failing executions.

In the long run, we expect automatic fix generation to rely on both search-based techniques (as in the approach of Weimer et al.) as well as specification mining (as in PACHIKA)—in addition to the wide range of information that is available via static analysis, theorem provers, bug history, and other techniques.

8.7.4 Repairing State

Demsky et al. [34] show how to automatically fix data structures at run-time, again according to a given specification. Rinard et al. [88] suggest similar repair techniques for invalid memory accesses. In both these works, only the program state is fixed. Weimer's and our work, though, look for repairs not only to the program state of the current run, but to its actual *code* (which as a side-effect yields repairs to the state as well). This requires many more checks, such as contracts or a regression test suite, but also increases confidence in the correctness of the repairs—besides, hopefully, providing a permanent fix to the problem.

8.7.5 Mining Specifications

PACHIKA is an instance of *specification mining* tools. The behavior models as mined by PACHIKA were first implemented in the ADABU tool [28]. The concept was later adapted by Ghezzi et al. [47]. Their ADIHEU tool uses models generated by ADABU to support recovering algebraic specifications from program runs. This approach could also be used in PACHIKA to capture object behavior and find anomalies.

Dynamic invariants, as conceived by Ernst et al. [39], express properties of data that hold at specific moments during the observed executions. By checking object attribute states, one could use the DAIKON [39] tool to extract pre- and postconditions for method calls and thus object behavior models.

The concept of learning models from actual program runs was first explored by Amons et al. [1], applying a probabilistic NFA learner on C traces. Their approach relies on manual annotations to relate functions to objects (such as C sockets or X11 selections) and to distinguish object definers from object users.

8.7.6 Generating Tests

Our work on generating fixes was heavily inspired by recent work on generating tests. Ciupa et al. [21] generate random sequences of method calls, leveraging existing contracts to retain only valid sequences. When a test case fails, the approach of Leitner et al. [64] automatically extracts a test case that reproduces the failure. Both generation and extraction of call sequences to characterize passing and failing runs are key concepts of PACHIKA.

8.8 Conclusions

Automatic generation of fixes as the natural next step after fix localization is an emerging field starting to gain momentum. We propose a new approach called PACHIKA that leverages object behavior models to analyze differences between normal and abnormal behavior. Our approach successfully constrains the search space to quickly generate potential fixes that not only remove the problem at hand, but also have a high diagnostic quality. In an evaluation with real bugs, PACHIKA was able to generate fixes that pass the test suite for five out of 53 bugs.

The technique can easily be extended to quality assurance beyond testing: As soon as a specification can be automatically validated, PACHIKA can leverage it to filter fix candidates.

Chapter 9
Conclusions and Future Work

What happens when a computer program runs? The answer can be frustratingly elusive, as anyone who has debugged or tuned a program knows. As it runs, a program overwrites its previous state, which might have provided a clue as to how the program got to the point at which it computed the wrong answer or otherwise failed. This all-too-common experience is symptomatic of a more general problem: the difficulty of accurately and efficiently capturing and analyzing the sequence of events that occur when a program executes.

– Thomas Ball/James R. Larus [6]

Capturing the dynamic behavior of a program is challenging. Even for short runs that last only a few seconds, a complete trace consists of several gigabytes of data. The sheer size of the trace file makes it difficult to analyze behavior based on this data. Hence, many applications represent dynamic information using different types of *software execution models*. A software execution model is an abstract representation of the trace file that captures those aspects of the dynamic behavior that are important for the application at hand. Existing types of software execution models mostly use only control-flow information.

This thesis has presented a novel type of software execution model called *object behavior models*, which characterize the behavior of individual objects at runtime. Such models are finite state automata where states represent different states of the object and transitions occur due to method invocations. An object behavior model describes the effect of a method invocation in terms of changes to the object's state. By combining control-flow with information about the values of variables, object behavior models capture important aspects of the dynamic behavior that are not represented by existing software execution models.

The contributions of this thesis are as follows:

- We have presented object behavior models, a novel approach to modeling the runtime behavior of object-oriented programs. To make the models concise, we use an abstraction function based on existing invariant categories further refined by static analysis that maps concrete values to abstract categories.

- We have described ADABU, a tool that mines object behavior models from the execution of

JAVA programs. Our implementation is robust and capable of mining models from the execution of large interactive programs such as ECLIPSE and ASPECTJ.

- We have presented IBUGS, an approach that mines bug benchmarks from the history of projects. Currently, the repository contains several hundreds of bugs mined from two large projects. The benchmark is publicly available so that other researchers can benefit from our work.

- We have shown that object behavior models can be used as specifications for the correct usage of a class. Our TAUTOKO tool uses ADABU to mine object behavior models from the execution of test suites. If the initial models do not provide enough coverage, TAUTOKO mutates the test suite to generate enriched specifications. When fed into a typestate verifier, enriched models are able to detect statistically significantly more bugs than initial models.

- We have presented an approach that automatically generates fix candidates for a given failure. Our PACHIKA tool uses ADABU to mine models from passing and failing runs and compares them to find violations of preconditions in the failing run. If a violation is found, PACHIKA analyzes the passing run models to propose patches that fix the violation. These candidate fixes are evaluated against the test suite, and PACHIKA proposes only those candidates that fix the problem and do not break any other tests. In a controlled experiment with the IBUGS subjects, ADABU was able to generate fixes that are semantically equivalent to fixes provided by the project developers.

In summary, this thesis advances the state of the art by introducing a new way to model dynamic program behavior which can be used as a basis for mining specifications and to synthesize fixes. To enable other researchers to benefit from this work, we have made the source code of all tools presented in this thesis available for download. The following sections present ideas for future work and instructions where to download each tool.

9.1 iBugs

The IBUGS repository is available for download at

> http://www.ibugs.org

Our next steps to improve the infrastructure will include the following:

Extend the repository. We plan to add more subjects to the IBUGS repository. In particular, we want to add projects that are multithreaded and provide a graphical user interface.

Classification of bugs. Our tags and fingerprint provide an initial classification of bugs. We plan to further improve this classification by using automated techniques from data mining. This will greatly improve the value of our data sets, because researchers can test for which kinds of bugs their tools perform best.

Score measure. In order to measure the success of bug localization tools, Renieris and Reiss introduced a *score* [86] that indicates the fraction of the code that can be ignored when searching for a bug. In future releases of our dataset, we want to provide a tool that computes this score. This will hopefully unify the assessment of results.

9.2 Tautoko

The source code and binary versions of TAUTOKO are available online at

> http://www.st.cs.uni-saarland.de/models/tautoko/

Future work on TAUTOKO will contain the following:

Technical Improvements. TAUTOKO can only apply one mutation at a time, which is why some states cannot be fully explored. This is due to limitations of the instrumentation framework. In the future, we would like to extend TAUTOKO such that arbitrary combinations of mutations are possible.

Test Case Generation. TAUTOKO's strategy for generating tests is simple but effective and only requires a test suite as input. However, there are many other approaches to test case generation that could be used just as well. One idea for future work is to compare different strategies in terms of their ability to enrich a specification.

9.3 Pachika

The project page for PACHIKA is available online at

> http://www.st.cs.uni-saarland.de/models/pachika/

There are several interesting ideas to further explore possibilities for automatically generating fixes:

Alternate differences. Right now, the set of differences we observe and the set of fixes we can generate is limited to conditional method calls. However, there are many more potential fixes that could be generated. For instance, assigning a value to an attribute could instantly fix the object state.

Adaptive fix generation. With a larger set of possible fixes, one could consider adaptive techniques to systematically explore the search space, as in the approach of Weimer et al. [107]. One interesting possibility could be to start with behavioral differences as fix candidates (as PACHIKA does), and to use these as a basis for further mutations.

Assessing the impact of fixes. What happens if there are multiple fix candidates that all pass the test suite? In this case, we also would like to minimize the *impact* on passing executions—impact as measured using dynamic invariants [93], coverage [49], or object behavior models.

Appendix A

Additional Figures and Tables

1. **Select bugs.** Use the meta information provided in the file *repository.xml* to select relevant bugs.

   Example: In order to select all bugs that raised a NullPointerException, use the XPath [112] expression

   /repository/bug[tag="null pointer exception"]

2. **Extract versions.** Use the ant task *checkoutversion*.

   Example: In order to checkout the pre-fix and post-fix versions for Bug 4711, type

   `ant -DfixId=4711 checkoutversion`

   The results are placed in the directory *"versions/4711/"*.

3. **Build the program.** Use the ant task *buildversion*.

   Example: Build the pre-fix version of Bug 4711 with

   `ant -DfixId=4711 -Dtag=pre-fix buildversion`

   If the build succeeds, you find the Jar files in the directory *".../pre-fix/org.aspectj/modules/aj-build/dist/tools/lib/"*

   Note: Static tools can analyze the Jars in this directory, while dynamic tools that execute tests need to instrument the Jars created in the next step.

4. **Build tests (dynamic tools).** Use the ant task *buildtests*.

   Example: In order to build the tests for the pre-fix version of Bug 4711, type

   `ant -DfixId=4711 -Dtag=pre-fix buildtests`

   This creates a Jar file that includes the ASPECTJ compiler and all resources needed for testing in the directory *"versions/4711/prefix/org.aspectj/modules/aj-build/jars/"*.

Figure A.1: Step-by-step guide for an evaluation based on IBUGS (1/2).

5. **Run test suites (dynamic tools).** Use the ant tasks *runharnesstests* for the integration test suite and *runjunittests* for the unit test suite of ASPECTJ, respectively.

    Example: Run unit tests for the pre-fix version of Bug 4711

    ```
    ant -DfixId=4711 -Dtag=pre-fix runjunittests
    ```

6. **Run specific tests (dynamic tools).** Generate scripts by using the ant task *gentestscript* and execute them.

    Example: In order to execute test *"SUID: thisJoinPoint"* described in file *"org.aspectj/modules/tests/ajcTests.xml"* generate a script with

    ```
    ant -DfixId=4711 -Dtag=pre-fix
    -DtestFileName="org.aspectj.modules/tests/ajcTests.xml"
    -DtestName="SUID: thisJoinPoint".
    ```

    This creates a new ant script in the directory *"4711/pre-fix/org.aspectj/modules/tests/"*. Execute this file to run test *"SUID: thisJoinPoint"*.

    Hint: All tests executed by the test suite are described in the file *"4711/pre-fix/testresults.xml"*.

7. **Assess your tool.** Compare the predicted bug location against the location changed in the fix (see *repository.xml*).

Figure A.2: Step-by-step guide for an evaluation based on IBUGS. Static bug localization tools typically integrate with Step 3 and 4. Dynamic tools need to run programs and therefore integrate with Step 4, 5, and 6.

```
1  for (int i = types.length - 1;
2       i >= 0; i--) {
3  -   if (typePattern.matchesExactly
4  -     (types[i])) return true;
5  +   if (typePattern.matchesStatically
6  +     (types[i])) return true;
7    }
8    return false;
```

Bug 42539: "throw derivative pointcuts not advised."

Figerprint: M Z-if

```
1   ResolvedTypeX[] parameterTypes =
2     searchStart.getWorld().resolve(..);
3
4  -   arguments = arguments.
5  -   resolveReferences(bindings);
6  +   TypePatternList arguments =
7  +     this.arguments.
8  +   resolveReferences(bindings);
9
10    IntMap newBindings=new IntMap();
```

Bug 43194: "java.lang.VerifyError in generated code"

Fingerprint: K-this M

```
1   if (getKind().isEnclosingKind()) {
2     return getSignature();
3  +   } else if (getKind() ==
4  +   Shadow.PreInitialization) {
5  +   // PreInit doesn't enclose code
6  +   // but its signature
7  +   // is correctly the signature
8  +   // of the ctor.
9  +   return getSignature();
10   } else if(enclosingShadow==null){
11     return getEnclosingMethod().
12     getMemberView();
```

Bug 67774: "Nullpointer-exception in pointcuts using withincode() clause"

Fingerprint: K-else K-if K-return M O-== Z-if

```
1   String packageName = StructureUtil.
2     getPackageDeclarationFromFile
3     (inputFile);
4
5  -   if (packageName != null ) {
6  +   if (packageName != null &&
7       packageName != "") {
8       writer.println( "package " +
9       packageName + ";" );
10    }
```

Bug 69011: "ajdoc fails when using default package"

Fingerprint: O-!= O-&& T V Y Z-if

Figure A.3: Examples for different bugs with fingerprints (1/3). Bug identifiers refer to the ASPECTJ project.

```
 1  if (shadow.getSourceLocation()
 2       == null
 3       || checker.getSourceLocation()
 4       == null)
 5    return;
 6
 7  + // Ensure a node for the target exists
 8  + IProgramElement targetNode =
 9  + getNode(...);
10  +
11    String sourceHandle = targetNode.
12      createHandleIdentifier(
13        checker.getSourceLocation().
14        getSourceFile(),
```

Bug 80916: "In some cases the structure model doesn't contain the matches declare relationship"

Fingerprint: M T V

```
 1  // matched by the typePattern.
 2  ResolvedType[] annTypes =
 3    annotated.getAnnotationTypes();
 4  - if (annTypes.length!=0) {
 5  + if (annTypes!=null &&
 6  +   annTypes.length!=0) {
 7      for (int i = 0;
 8        i < annTypes.length;
 9        i++) {
```

Bug 123695: "Internal nullptr exception with complex declare annotation statement that affects injected methods"

Fingerprint: K-null O-!= O-&& T V Z-if

```
 1      }
 2    }
 3  - if (it.hasNext())
 4  -   sb.append(", ");
 5  + if (it.hasNext())
 6  +   sb.append(",");
 7    }
 8    sb.append(')');
```

Bug 132130: "Missing relationship for declare @method when annotating a co-located method"

Fingerprint: Y

Figure A.4: Examples for different bugs with fingerprints (2/3). Bug identifiers refer to the ASPECTJ project.

```
1   try {
2  + synchronized (loader) {
3       WeavingAdaptor weavingAdaptor =
4         WeaverContainer.getWeaver(...);
5       if (weavingAdaptor == null) {
6         if (trace.isTraceEnabled())
7           trace.exit("preProcess",
8                       bytes);
9         return bytes;
10      }
11      return weavingAdaptor.
12        weaveClass(className, bytes);
13 + }
14 } catch (Exception t) {
15     trace.error("preProcess",t);
```

Bug 151182: "NPE in BcelWeaver using LTW"

Fingerprint: K-synchronized T V

```
1   // at the moment it only deals with
2   // 'declared exception is not thrown'
3   if (!shadow.getWorld().
4       isIgnoringUnusedThrownException()
5  -    && !thrownExceptions.isEmpty()) {
6  +    && !getThrownExceptions().
7  +    isEmpty()) {
8       Member member =
9         shadow.getSignature();
10      if (member instanceof
11          BcelMethod) {
```

Bug 161217: "NPE in BcelAdvice"

Fingerprint: Z-if

Figure A.5: Examples for different bugs with fingerprints (3/3). Bug identifiers refer to the ASPECTJ project.

```xml
<bug id="69459">
  <property name="files-churned" value="1"/>
  <property name="java-files-churned" value="1"/>
  <property name="classes-churned" value="1"/>
  <property name="methods-churned" value="1"/>
  <property name="hunks" value="3"/>
  <property name="lines-added" value="0"/>
  <property name="lines-deleted" value="0"/>
  <property name="lines-modified" value="11"/>
  <property name="lines-churned" value="11"/>
  <property name="priority" value="P3"/>
  <property name="severity" value="normal"/>
  <concisefingerprint>KMZ</concisefingerprint>
  <fullfingerprint>K-else K-if K-null M O-! O-&amp;&amp;
  O-+ T V Y Z-if</fullfingerprint>
  <pre-fix-testcases failing="105" passing="1203"/>
  <post-fix-testcases failing="105" passing="1204"/>
  <testsforfix type="new">
    <file location="ajcTests.xml">
      <test name="Hiding_of_Instance_Methods"/>
    </file>
  </testsforfix>
  <fixedFiles>
    <file name="ResolvedTypex.java" revision="1.27">
...
1194c1194,1202
&lt;
---
&gt; if (parent.isStatic()
&gt; &amp;&amp; !child.isStatic()) {
...
    </file>
  </fixedFiles>
</bug>
```

Figure A.6: XML content descriptor for bug 69459.

Appendix B

Trace File Format Description

This chapter describes the trace file format as processed by the ADABU model miner. The purpose of this chapter is to provide enough information to implement a language frontend that generates a trace file.

B.1 Concepts

The trace file was designed with the following goals in mind:

Simplicity The existing JAVA implementation uses sophisticated instrumentation techniques to gather the required information. As instrumentation in JAVA is very fragile, instrumentation and tracing is kept as simple as possible.

Self-Containedness The trace file is self-contained, i.e. it contains all information in one single file.

Events The trace file essentially is a sequence of *events*. Each event describes an action in the run that is of interest to ADABU.

Independence The event types are designed for a maximum of independence between events that deal with different aspects of the execution. For example, it is possible to completely turn off tracing of array operations.

Stream processing ADABU only reads the trace file once and does not jump between different locations in the trace file. This requires that information in the trace file respects a certain order. At least for JAVA, this can sometimes be difficult.

Record Everything Sometimes it is difficult to reproduce exactly the same execution due to different schedules for the garbage collector and other issues. To avoid those problems, the existing tracer records as much information as possible for as many objects as possible.

Identifiers For efficiency reasons, the trace file makes heavy use of identifiers. For example, the name and signature of a method m are only transmitted once. All subsequent invocations of m only specify an identifier for the method.

B.1.1 Serialization

The existing implementation serializes data using JAVA's `DataOutputStream` class. This is a low-level serialization class that provides methods for writing all primitive JAVA types. To read the data, the corresponding `DataInputStream` class can be used. In order to be processed by AD-ABU, the trace file has to use the same serialization scheme as `DataOutputStream`. Porting `DataOutputStream` to another language should be fairly easy.

B.1.2 Object Identifiers

To mine models, ADABU needs to be able to identify the target object for field accesses and method invocations. To achieve this, all events associated with a target object specify an identifier (a positive integer) for the target object. This identifier must be unique among all objects and remain unchanged over the life-time of the object. An object's identifier is established right after the object was created and before the constructor is invoked.

B.1.3 Method Identifiers

A method identifier is a positive integer that identifies a method in a unique manner. Similar to object identifiers, method identifiers have to be specified in the trace file before the first use.

B.1.4 Field Identifiers

A field identifier is a positive integer that identifies a field in a unique manner. Field identifiers also have to be specified before they are used for the first time.

B.1.5 Thread Identifiers

ADABU is able to distinguish events in different threads. To do so, ADABU requires almost all events to specify an identifier for the thread that caused the event. Just like the other identifier types, thread identifiers are positive integers that uniquely identify a thread.

B.1.6 Allocation Site Identifiers

For some analyzes, ADABU needs to distinguish different allocation sites in a method. The new object event B.2.1 therefore also specifies an integer that uniquely identifies the allocation site within the method.

B.1.7 Invocation Site Identifiers

In some circumstances, ADABU needs to know exactly where a call to a method came from. To do so, the invocation site event B.2.2 specifies a positive identifier that uniquely identifies the code position where the method call came from.

B.2 Events

This section describes all possible events in the trace file. Every event writes the following two values as its first values:

name	type	description
eventId	byte	An identifier for the event type. A list of event identifiers can be found in Table B.1
threadId	integer	An identifier for the thread that caused the event (see Section B.1.5).

B.2.1 Identifier Events

Method Identifier Events

This event specifies the identifier for a certain method. The event has to occur before any other event that uses the method identifier. It specifies the following values:

name	type	description
methodId	integer	A positive integer that uniquely identifies the method.
methodName	utf8	A serialized representation of the method name (see below).

A method identifier is serialized as follows:

1. The fully qualified class name that contains the method with slashes instead of dots as separator for the package levels.

2. A dot.

3. The name of the method.

4. The signature of the method as specified by the JAVA virtual machine specification [68].

5. A hash.

6. The access modifier encoded as specified by the ASM documentation [82].

Field Identifier Events

This event specifies the identifier for a certain field. The event has to occur before any other event that uses it.

name	type	description
fieldId	integer	A positive integer that uniquely identifies the field.
fieldName	utf8	A serialized representation of the field name (see below).

A field identifier is serialized as follows:

1. The fully qualified class name that contains the method with slashes instead of dots as separator for the package levels.
2. A percentage sign.
3. The name of the field.
4. A percentage sign.
5. The type of the field as specified by the JAVA virtual machine specification [68].
6. A percentage sign.
7. A serialized boolean (`true` or `false`) indicating whether or not the field is static.

Class Identifier Events

This event specifies an identifier for a class. It has to occur before any other event that uses it.

name	type	description
classId	integer	A positive integer that uniquely identifies the class.
className	utf8	The fully qualified class name with slashes instead of dots.

Object Created Events

This event indicates that a new object was created. It has occur before any other event that is associated with the object. In particular, it also has to occur before the first call to a constructor.

name	type	description
objectId	integer	The identifier for the new object.
classId	integer	The identifier for the runtime class of the new object.
allocationSiteId	integer	The identifier for the allocation site (see Section B.1.6).

Array Created Events

This event indicates that a new array was created. It is similar to the object created event described in Section B.2.1. In JAVA, arrays are also objects and therefore also get an identifier. For multi-dimensional arrays, the trace must contain array create events (and array write events, see Section B.2.6) for all arrays created.

name	type	description
arrayId	integer	The identifier for the new array.
typeDesc	utf8	The type description for the new array as specified by the virtual machine specification [68].
allocationSiteId	integer	The identifier for the allocation site (see Section B.1.6).

B.2.2 Method Call Events

Method Start Event

This event indicates that the execution of a method has started. It has to occur before any other event that happens when the method is active.

name	type	description
methodId	integer	The identifier for the method.
objectId	integer	The identifier of the target object for the call or -2 if this is a static method.

Regular Method End Event

This event indicates the end of a method. It has to be the last event that is traced when the method is active. This event indicates a regular method end, i.e. the method returned normally and did not raise an exception.

name	type	description
methodId	integer	The identifier for the method.

Exceptional Method End Event

This event indicates a method end that raised an exception. It has to be the last event that is traced when the method is active.

name	type	description
methodId	integer	The identifier for the method.
exceptionClass	utf8	The fully qualified class name of the exception that was raised with slashes instead of dots.

Invocation Site Event

This event specifies the invocation site for a call (see Section B.1.7). It has to occur right before the corresponding method start event.

name	type	description
siteId	integer	The identifier for the invocation site.

B.2.3 Parameter Events

A parameter event specifies the value that was passed as a parameter to the currently active method. Parameter events occur right after the corresponding method start event. Similar to field events, there is one event type for each primitive type and one for complex types (see Table B.1).

name	type	description
index	integer	The index of the parameter.
value	see description	The value of the parameter. For primitive types, this is simply the serialized value. For complex types, the value is the object identifier passed as an integer.

B.2.4 Return Events

A return event specifies the value that was returned by a method invocation. Return events occur right before the corresponding method end event. There is one return event for all 32 bit integer types (for JAVA these are `boolean, byte, char, short` and `int`), one return event for `void` methods, return event types for the remaining primitive types and one for complex return values.

name	type	description
value	see description	The returned value. For primitive types, this is simply the serialized value. For complex types, the value is the object identifier passed as an integer.

B.2.5 Field Access Events

This section summarizes all events that indicate read or write access to a field.

Field Read Events

A field read event occurs if the value of a class field is read by a method. All field read events specify the same values:

name	type	description
objectId	integer	The identifier for the object the field belongs to or -2 if this is a static field.
fieldId	integer	The identifier of the field that was read.
value	see description	The value that was read from the field. For fields of primitive type, this is simply the serialized value of the field. For fields of complex type, the value is the object identifier passed as an integer.

Table B.1 lists all field read events. Basically, there is one event type for each primitive type, and one for complex types.

Field Write Events

A field write event occurs if the value of a class field is written by a method. All field write events specify the same values:

name	type	description
objectId	integer	The identifier for the object the field belongs to or -2 if this is a static field.
fieldId	integer	The identifier of the field that was written.
value	see description	The value that was written to the field. For fields of primitive type, this is simply the serialized value of the field. For fields of complex type, the value is the object identifier passed as an integer.

Table B.1 lists all field write events. Basically, there is one event type for each primitive type, and one for complex types.

B.2.6 Array Access Events

Although arrays are in many ways similar to objects, ADABU has separate events for arrays to allow for independent tracing of objects and arrays.

Array Read Events

An array read event occurs if the value of an array is read by a method. All array read events specify the same values:

name	type	description
arrayId	integer	The identifier for the array.
index	integer	The index in the array that was accessed.
value	see description	The value that was read from the array. For arrays of primitive type, this is simply the serialized value. For arrays of complex type, the value is the object identifier passed as an integer.

Table B.1 lists all array read events. Basically, there is one event type for each primitive type, and one for complex types.

Array Write Events

An array write event occurs if the value of a class field is written by a method. All array write events specify the same values:

name	type	description
arrayId	integer	The identifier for the array.
index	integer	The index in the array that was accessed.
value	see description	The value that was written to the array. For arrays of primitive type, this is simply the serialized value. For arrays of complex type, the value is the object identifier passed as an integer.

B.2.7 Inspector Events

ADABU supports using return values of inspectors in the state representation. To this end, the user has to specify an XML file with a list of inspectors. At trace time, ADABU reads this file and injects additional calls to inspectors at the beginning and the end of every non-inspector (and non-static) method. Return values are then written to the stream using events 62 to 66.

name	type	description
objectId	integer	The identifier for the target object.
methodId	integer	The identifier for the inspector.
value		The value that was returned by the inspector. For inspectors with primitive return values, this is simply the serialized value. For inspectors with complex return type, the value is the object identifier passed as an integer.

B.2.8 List of Event Identifiers

Table B.1 lists all field write events. Basically, there is one event type for each primitive type, and one for complex types.

name	Id		name	Id
EV_METHODNAME	2		EV_ARRAYWRITE_OBJECT	36
EV_FIELDNAME	3		EV_EX_METHODEND	37
EV_CLASSNAME	4		EV_ASTORE	38
EV_METHODSTART	5		EV_FIELDREAD_BOOLEAN	39
EV_METHODEND	6		EV_FIELDREAD_BYTE	40
EV_CALLSITE	7		EV_FIELDREAD_SHORT	41
EV_FIELDWRITE_BOOLEAN	8		EV_FIELDREAD_CHAR	42
EV_FIELDWRITE_BYTE	9		EV_FIELDREAD_INT	43
EV_FIELDWRITE_SHORT	10		EV_FIELDREAD_LONG	44
EV_FIELDWRITE_CHAR	11		EV_FIELDREAD_FLOAT	45
EV_FIELDWRITE_INT	12		EV_FIELDREAD_DOUBLE	46
EV_FIELDWRITE_LONG	13		EV_FIELDREAD_OBJECT	47
EV_FIELDWRITE_FLOAT	14		EV_PURGE	48
EV_FIELDWRITE_DOUBLE	15		EV_PARAMETER_BOOL	49
EV_FIELDWRITE_OBJECT	16		EV_PARAMETER_BYTE	50
EV_PARAMETER_OBJECT	17		EV_PARAMETER_SHORT	51
EV_OBJECTCREATED	18		EV_PARAMETER_CHAR	52
EV_ARRAYCREATED	20		EV_PARAMETER_INT	53
EV_ARRAYREAD_BYTE	21		EV_PARAMETER_LONG	54
EV_ARRAYREAD_SHORT	22		EV_PARAMETER_FLOAT	55
EV_ARRAYREAD_CHAR	23		EV_PARAMETER_DOUBLE	56
EV_ARRAYREAD_INT	24		EV_RETURN_OBJECT	19
EV_ARRAYREAD_LONG	25		EV_RETURN_INT	57
EV_ARRAYREAD_FLOAT	26		EV_RETURN_FLOAT	58
EV_ARRAYREAD_DOUBLE	27		EV_RETURN_LONG	59
EV_ARRAYREAD_OBJECT	28		EV_RETURN_DOUBLE	60
EV_ARRAYWRITE_BYTE	29		EV_RETURN_VOID	61
EV_ARRAYWRITE_SHORT	30		EV_INSPECTOR_INT	62
EV_ARRAYWRITE_CHAR	31		EV_INSPECTOR_FLOAT	63
EV_ARRAYWRITE_INT	32		EV_INSPECTOR_LONG	64
EV_ARRAYWRITE_LONG	33		EV_INSPECTOR_DOUBLE	65
EV_ARRAYWRITE_FLOAT	34		EV_INSPECTOR_OBJECT	66
EV_ARRAYWRITE_DOUBLE	35			

Table B.1: A list of all event identifiers processed by ADABU.

Bibliography

[1] AMMONS, G., BODÍK, R., AND LARUS, J. Mining Specifications. In *Conference Record of POPL'02: the 29th ACM SIGPLAN-SIGACT Symposium on Principles of Programming Languages* (Portland, Oregon, Jan. 16–18, 2002), pp. 4–16.

[2] ANVIK, J., HIEW, L., AND MURPHY, G. C. Who Should Fix this Bug? In *ICSE '06: Proceeding of the 28th International Conference on Software Engineering* (New York, NY, USA, 2006), ACM Press, pp. 361–370.

[3] ARTZI, S., KIEZUN, A., GLASSER, D., AND ERNST, M. D. Combined Static and Dynamic Mutability Analysis. In *ASE '07: Proceedings of the twenty-second IEEE/ACM International Conference on Automated Software Engineering* (2007), ACM, pp. 104–113.

[4] ARTZI, S., KIM, S., AND ERNST, M. D. ReCrash: Making Software Failures Reproducible by Preserving Object States. In *ECOOP 2008 — Object-Oriented Programming, 22nd European Conference* (Paphos, Cyprus, July 9–11, 2008), pp. 542–565.

[5] AT&T. Graphviz Graph Visualization. http://www.graphviz.org/ as of 04-07-2010.

[6] BALL, T., AND LARUS, J. R. Using Paths to Measure, Explain, and Enhance Program Behavior. *Computer 33*, 7 (2000), 57–65.

[7] BANNING, J. P. An Efficient Way to Find the Side Effects of Procedure Calls and the Aliases of Variables. In *POPL '79: Proceedings of the 6th ACM SIGACT-SIGPLAN Symposium on Principles of Programming languages* (1979), ACM, pp. 29–41.

[8] BARNETT, M., DELINE, R., FÄHNDRICH, M., JACOBS, B., LEINO, K. R., SCHULTE, W., AND VENTER, H. The Spec# Programming System: Challenges and Directions. In *Verified Software: Theories, Tools, Experiments: First IFIP TC 2/WG 2.3 Conference, VSTTE 2005, Zurich, Switzerland, October 10-13, 2005, Revised Selected Papers and Discussions* (Berlin, Heidelberg, 2008), Springer-Verlag, pp. 144–152.

[9] BERTOLINO, A., INVERARDI, P., PELLICCIONE, P., AND TIVOLI, M. Automatic Synthesis of Behavior Protocols for Composable Web-services. In *ESEC/FSE '09: Proceedings of the 7th Joint Meeting of the European Software Engineering Conference and the ACM SIGSOFT Symposium on the Foundations of Software Engineering* (New York, NY, USA, 2009), ACM, pp. 141–150.

[10] BIERHOFF, K., AND ALDRICH, J. Modular Typestate Checking of Aliased Objects. In *OOPSLA '07: Proceedings of the 22nd annual ACM SIGPLAN Conference on Object-oriented Programming Systems and applications* (New York, NY, USA, 2007), ACM, pp. 301–320.

[11] BIERMANN, A. W., AND FELDMAN, J. A. On the Synthesis of Finite-State Machines from Samples of Their Behavior. *IEEE Transactions Comput. 21*, 6 (1972), 592–597.

[12] BIRD, C., BACHMANN, A., AUNE, E., DUFFY, J., BERNSTEIN, A., FILKOV, V., AND DEVANBU, P. Fair and Balanced?: Bias in Bug-fix Datasets. In *ESEC/FSE '09: Proceedings of the 7th Joint Meeting of the European Software Engineering Conference and the ACM SIGSOFT Symposium on the Foundations of Software Engineering on European Software Engineering Conference and Foundations of Software Engineering Symposium* (New York, NY, USA, 2009), ACM, pp. 121–130.

[13] BLACKBURN, S. M., GARNER, R., HOFFMANN, C., KHANG, A. M., MCKINLEY, K. S., BENTZUR, R., DIWAN, A., FEINBERG, D., FRAMPTON, D., GUYER, S. Z., HIRZEL, M., HOSKING, A., JUMP, M., LEE, H., MOSS, J. E. B., MOSS, B., PHANSALKAR, A., STEFANOVIĆ, D., VANDRUNEN, T., VON DINCKLAGE, D., AND WIEDERMANN, B. The dacapo benchmarks: java benchmarking development and analysis. In *OOPSLA '06: Proceedings of the 21st annual ACM SIGPLAN conference on Object-oriented programming systems, languages, and applications* (New York, NY, USA, 2006), ACM, pp. 169–190.

[14] BORTZ, J. *Statistik für Sozialwissenschaftler*, 4 ed. Springer, Berlin [u.a.], 1993.

[15] BOWRING, J. F., REHG, J. M., AND HARROLD, M. J. Active Learning for Automatic Classification of Software Behavior. In *ISSTA '04: Proceedings of the 2004 ACM SIGSOFT International Symposium on Software Testing and Analysis* (New York, NY, USA, 2004), ACM, pp. 195–205.

[16] BRANDES, U. GraphML XML Graph File Format. http://graphml.graphdrawing.org/ as of 04-07-2010.

[17] BRIAND, L. C. A Critical Analysis of Empirical Research in Software Testing. In *ESEM '07: Proceedings of the First International Symposium on Empirical Software Engineering and Measurement* (Washington, DC, USA, 2007), IEEE Computer Society, pp. 1–8.

[18] BURGER, M. Locating Failure-Inducing Code Changes in an Industrial Environment. Diploma thesis, Saarland University, December 2005.

[19] CATANO, N., AND HUISMAN, M. CHASE: A Static Checker for JML's Assignable Clause. In *VMCAI 2003: Proceedings of the 4th International Conference on Verification, Model Checking, and Abstract Interpretation* (2003), Springer-Verlag, pp. 26–40.

[20] CHIBA, S. Javassist 3.2. http://www.jboss.org/javassist as of 07-05-2010.

[21] CIUPA, I., LEITNER, A., ORIOL, M., AND MEYER, B. Experimental Assessment of Random Testing for Object-oriented Software. In *ISSTA '07: Proceedings of the 2007 International Symposium on Software Testing and Analysis* (New York, NY, USA, 2007), ACM, pp. 84–94.

[22] CLEVE, H., AND ZELLER, A. Locating Causes of Program Failures. In *Proceedings of the 27th International Conference on Software Engineering (ICSE 2005)* (St. Louis, USA, 2005).

[23] COOK, J., AND WOLF, A. Discovering Models of Software Processes from Event-Based Data. *ACM Transactions on Software Engineering and Methodology 7*, 3 (July 1998), 215–249.

[24] COOPER, K. D., AND KENNEDY, K. Interprocedural Side-effect Analysis in Linear Time. In *PLDI '88: Proceedings of the ACM SIGPLAN 1988 Conference on Programming Language design and Implementation* (1988), ACM, pp. 57–66.

[25] CUBRANIC, D., MURPHY, G. C., SINGER, J., AND BOOTH, K. S. Hipikat: A Project Memory for Software Development. *IEEE Transactions on Software Engineering 31*, 6 (June 2005), 446–465.

[26] DAHM, M. Byte Code Engineering with the Java API. Technical Report B-17-98, Freie Universität Berlin, Institut für Informatik, Berlin, Germany, July 07 1999.

[27] DALLMEIER, V., KNOPP, N., MALLON, C., HACK, S., AND ZELLER, A. Generating test cases for specification mining. In *ISSTA '10: Proceedings of the 19th International Symposium on Software Testing and Analysis* (New York, NY, USA, 2010), ACM, pp. 85–96.

[28] DALLMEIER, V., LINDIG, C., WASYLKOWSKI, A., AND ZELLER, A. Mining Object Behavior with ADABU. In *WODA '06: Proceedings of the 2006 International Workshop on Dynamic Systems Analysis* (New York, NY, USA, 2006), ACM, pp. 17–24.

[29] DALLMEIER, V., LINDIG, C., AND ZELLER, A. Lightweight Defect Localization for Java. In *European Conference on Object-Oriented Programming (ECOOP)* (2005), A. Black, Ed.

[30] DALLMEIER, V., ZELLER, A., AND MEYER, B. Generating Fixes from Object Behavior Anomalies. *Automated Software Engineering, International Conference on* (2009), 550–554.

[31] DALLMEIER, V., AND ZIMMERMANN, T. Extraction of Bug Localization Benchmarks from History. In *ASE '07: Proceedings of the twenty-second IEEE/ACM International Conference on Automated Software Engineering* (New York, NY, USA, 2007), ACM, pp. 433–436.

[32] DELINE, R., AND FÄHNDRICH, M. Typestates for Objects. In *In Proceedings 18th ECOOP* (2004), Springer, pp. 465–490.

[33] DEMILLO, R. A., LIPTON, R. J., AND SAYWARD, F. G. Hints on Test Data Selection: Help for the Practicing Programmer. *Computer 11*, 4 (1978), 34–41.

[34] DEMSKY, B., AND RINARD, M. Data Structure Repair using Goal-directed Reasoning. In *ICSE '05: Proceedings of the 27th International Conference on Software Engineering* (New York, NY, USA, 2005), ACM, pp. 176–185.

[35] DIETZ, F. Ristretto 1.0. http://ostatic.com/ristretto as of 01-12-2010.

[36] DIETZ, L., DALLMEIER, V., ZELLER, A., AND SCHEFFER, T. Localizing Bugs in Program Executions with Graphical Model. In *Advances in Neural Information Processing Systems* (2009).

[37] DO, H., ELBAUM, S. G., AND ROTHERMEL, G. Supporting Controlled Experimentation with Testing Techniques: An Infrastructure and its Potential Impact. *Empirical Software Engineering: An International Journal 10*, 4 (2005), 405–435.

[38] ECLIPSE FOUNDATION. Eclipse GPL, 2008. http://www.eclipse.org/.

[39] ERNST, M. D., COCKRELL, J., GRISWOLD, W. G., AND NOTKIN, D. Dynamically Discovering Likely Program Invariants to Support Program Evolution. *IEEE Transactions on Software Engineering 27*, 2 (Feb. 2001), 1–25. A previous version appeared in *ICSE '99, Proceedings of the 21st International Conference on Software Engineering*, pages 213–224, Los Angeles, CA, USA, May 19–21, 1999.

[40] FINK, S. J., YAHAV, E., DOR, N., RAMALINGAM, G., AND GEAY, E. Effective Typestate Verification in the Presence of Aliasing. *ACM Transactions Software Engineering Methodology 17*, 2 (2008), 1–34.

[41] FISCHER, M., PINZGER, M., AND GALL, H. Populating a Release History Database from Version Control and Bug Tracking Systems. In *Proceedings International Conference on Software Maintenance (ICSM 2003)* (Amsterdam, Netherlands, Sept. 2003), IEEE.

[42] FOWLER, M. *Refactoring: Improving the Design of Existing Code*. Addison-Wesley Longman Publishing Co., Inc., Boston, MA, USA, 1999.

[43] FROST, R. Jazz and the Eclipse Way of Collaboration. *IEEE Software 24*, 6 (2007), 114–117.

[44] GAMMA, E. JUnit 3.8.1 GPL, 2007.

[45] GAMMA, E., HELM, R., JOHNSON, R., AND VLISSIDES, J. Design Patterns: Abstraction and Reuse of Object-Oriented Design, 1993.

[46] GEAY, E., YAHAV, E., AND FINK, S. Continuous Code-quality Assurance with SAFE. In *PEPM '06: Proceedings of the 2006 ACM SIGPLAN Symposium on Partial evaluation and semantics-based program manipulation* (New York, NY, USA, 2006), ACM Press, pp. 145–149.

[47] GHEZZI, C., MOCCI, A., AND MONGA, M. Efficient Recovery of Algebraic Specifications for Stateful Components. In *IWPSE '07: Ninth International Workshop on Principles of Software evolution* (New York, NY, USA, 2007), ACM, pp. 98–105.

[48] GOLD, E. Language Identification in the Limit. *Information and Control* (1967), 447–474.

[49] GRÜN, B. J. M., SCHULER, D., AND ZELLER, A. The Impact of Equivalent Mutants. In *ICSTW '09: Proceedings of the IEEE International Conference on Software Testing, Verification, and Validation Workshops* (Washington, DC, USA, 2009), IEEE Computer Society, pp. 192–199.

[50] GUPTA, N., AND HEIDEPRIEM, Z. V. A New Structural Coverage Criterion for Dynamic Detection of Program Invariants. *Automated Software Engineering, International Conference on 0* (2003), 49.

[51] HANGAL, S., AND LAM, M. S. Tracking Down software Bugs using Automatic Anomaly Detection. In *ICSE '02: Proceedings of the 24th International Conference on Software Engineering* (New York, NY, USA, 2002), ACM Press, pp. 291–301.

[52] HARROLD, M. J., ROTHERMEL, G., WU, R., AND YI, L. An Empirical Investigation of Program Spectra. In *PASTE '98: Proceedings of the 1998 ACM SIGPLAN-SIGSOFT Workshop on Program Analysis for Software Tools and Engineering* (New York, NY, USA, 1998), ACM, pp. 83–90.

[53] HIERONS, R. M., BOGDANOV, K., BOWEN, J. P., CLEAVELAND, R., DERRICK, J., DICK, J., GHEORGHE, M., HARMAN, M., KAPOOR, K., KRAUSE, P., AND LÜTTGEN, G. Using Formal Specifications to Support Testing. *ACM Comput. Surv. 41*, 2 (2009), 1–76.

[54] HOVEMEYER, D., AND PUGH, W. Finding Bugs is Easy. *SIGPLAN Not. 39*, 12 (2004), 92–106.

[55] INFO ETHER. PMD. http://pmd.sourceforge.net/.

[56] JHA, S., TAN, K., AND MAXION, R. A. Markov Chains, Classifiers, and Intrusion Detection. In *CSFW '01: Proceedings of the 14th IEEE Workshop on Computer Security Foundations* (Washington, DC, USA, 2001), IEEE Computer Society, p. 206.

[57] JONES, J. A., AND HARROLD, M. J. Empirical Evaluation of the Tarantula Automatic Fault-localization Technique. In *ASE '05: Proceedings of the 20th IEEE/ACM International Conference on Automated Software Engineering* (New York, NY, USA, 2005), ACM, pp. 273–282.

[58] Java Virtual Machine Tool Interface. http://java.sun.com/javase/6/docs/technotes/guides/jvmti/.

[59] KICZALES, G., HILSDALE, E., HUGUNIN, J., KERSTEN, M., PALM, J., AND GRISWOLD, W. G. An Overview of AspectJ. In *Proceedings of the 15th European Conference on Object-Oriented Programming (ECOOP)* (2001), J. L. Knudsen, Ed., vol. 2072 of *Lecture Notes in Computer Science*, pp. 327–353.

[60] KING, J. C. Symbolic Execution and Program Testing. *Commun. ACM 19*, 7 (1976), 385–394.

[61] KNIZHNIK, K., AND ARTHO, C. Jlint–Find bugs in Java programs. http://jlint.sourceforge.net/.

[62] KO, A. J., AND MYERS, B. A. A Framework and Methodology for Studying the Causes of Software Errors in Programming Systems. *Journal of Visual Languages and Computing 16*, 1-2 (2005), 41–84.

[63] KO, A. J., AND MYERS, B. A. Debugging Reinvented: Asking and Answering Why and Why Not Questions about Program Behavior. In *ICSE '08: Proceedings of the 30th International Conference on Software Engineering* (New York, NY, USA, 2008), ACM, pp. 301–310.

[64] LEITNER, A., CIUPA, I., ORIOL, M., MEYER, B., AND FIVA, A. Contract Driven Development = Test Driven Development - Writing Test Cases. In *ESEC-FSE '07: Proceedings of the ACM Symposium on the Foundations of Software Engineering* (New York, NY, USA, 2007), ACM, pp. 425–434.

[65] LI, Z., TAN, L., WANG, X., LU, S., ZHOU, Y., AND ZHAI, C. Have Things Changed Now?: An Empirical Study of Bug Characteristics in Modern Open Source Software. In *ASID '06: Proceedings of the 1st Workshop on Architectural and System support for improving Software dependability* (New York, NY, USA, 2006), ACM Press, pp. 25–33.

[66] LI, Z., AND ZHOU, Y. PR-Miner: Automatically Extracting Implicit Programming Rules and Detecting Violations in Large Software Code. In *ESEC/FSE-13: Proceedings of the 10th European Software Engineering Conference held jointly with 13th ACM SIGSOFT International Symposium on Foundations of Software Engineering* (New York, NY, USA, 2005), ACM Press, pp. 306–315.

[67] LIBLIT, B., NAIK, M., ZHENG, A. X., AIKEN, A., AND JORDAN, M. I. Scalable Statistical Bug Isolation. In *PLDI '05: Proceedings of the 2005 ACM SIGPLAN Conference on Programming language design and implementation* (New York, NY, USA, 2005), ACM Press, pp. 15–26.

[68] LINDHOLM, T., AND YELLIN, F. *The Java Virtual Machine Specification*, 1st ed. Addison-Wesley, Reading, Massachusetts, 1997.

[69] LIU, C., YAN, X., FEI, L., HAN, J., AND MIDKIFF, S. P. SOBER: Statistical Model-based Bug Localization. In *ESEC/FSE-13: Proceedings of the 10th European Software Engineering Conference held jointly with 13th ACM SIGSOFT International Symposium on Foundations of Software Engineering* (New York, NY, USA, 2005), ACM Press, pp. 286–295.

[70] LORENZOLI, D., MARIANI, L., AND PEZZÈ, M. Automatic Generation of Software Behavioral Models. In *ICSE '08: Proceedings of the 30th International Conference on Software Engineering* (New York, NY, USA, 2008), ACM, pp. 501–510.

[71] LU, S., LI, Z., QIN, F., TAN, L., ZHOU, P., AND ZHOU, Y. BugBench: Benchmarks for Evaluating Bug Detection Tools. In *PLDI Workshop on the Evaluation of Software Defect Detection Tools* (June 2005).

[72] MAJUMDAR, R., AND SEN, K. Hybrid Concolic Testing. In *ICSE '07: Proceedings of the 29th International Conference on Software Engineering* (Washington, DC, USA, 2007), IEEE Computer Society, pp. 416–426.

[73] MCMINN, P. Search-based Software Test Data Generation: A Survey. *Software Testing, Verification and Reliability 14* (2004), 105–156.

[74] MESBAH, A., AND VAN DEURSEN, A. Invariant-based Automatic Testing of AJAX User Interfaces. In *ICSE '09: Proceedings of the 2009 IEEE 31st International Conference on Software Engineering* (Washington, DC, USA, 2009), IEEE Computer Society, pp. 210–220.

[75] MEYER, B., FIVA, A., CIUPA, I., LEITNER, A., WEI, Y., AND STAPF, E. Programs That Test Themselves. *Computer 42* (2009), 46–55.

[76] MILANOVA, A., ROUNTEV, A., AND RYDER, B. G. Parameterized Object Sensitivity for Points-to and Side-effect Analyses for Java. *SIGSOFT Software Engineering Notes 27*, 4 (2002), 1–11.

[77] MILICEVIC, A., MISAILOVIC, S., MARINOV, D., AND KHURSHID, S. Korat: A Tool for Generating Structurally Complex Test Inputs. In *ICSE '07: Proceedings of the 29th International Conference on Software Engineering* (Washington, DC, USA, 2007), IEEE Computer Society, pp. 771–774.

[78] MOZILLA FOUNDATION. Rhino Javascript Interpreter. http://www.mozilla.org/rhino/ as of 01-28-2010.

[79] NATIONAL INSTITUTE OF STANDARDS. Software Errors Cost U.S. Economy $59.5 Billion Annually. http://www.nist.gov/publicaffairs/releases/n02-10.htm.

[80] NEUHAUS, S. *Repeating the Past: Experimental and Empirical Methods in System and Software Security*. PhD thesis, Saarland University, Department of Computer Science, 2008.

[81] NEUHAUS, S., AND ZELLER, A. Isolating Intrusions by Automatic Experiments. In *Proceedings of the 13th Annual Network and Distributed System Security Symposium* (Reston, VA, USA, February 2006), Internet Society, pp. 71–80.

[82] OBJECTWEB. ASM 3.2. http://asm.objectweb.org as of 12-01-2009.

[83] PRADEL, M., AND GROSS, T. R. Automatic Generation of Object Usage Specifications from Large Method Traces. *Automated Software Engineering, International Conference on 0* (2009), 371–382.

[84] PURUSHOTHAMAN, R., AND PERRY, D. E. Towards Understanding the Rhetoric of Small Source Code Changes. *IEEE Transactions on Software Engineering 31*, 6 (2005), 511–526.

[85] RAMANATHAN, M. K., GRAMA, A., AND JAGANNATHAN, S. Static Specification Inference using Predicate Mining. In *PLDI '07: Proceedings of the 2007 ACM SIGPLAN Conference on Programming language design and implementation* (New York, NY, USA, 2007), ACM, pp. 123–134.

[86] RENIERIS, M., AND REISS, S. P. Fault Localization With Nearest Neighbor Queries. In *Proceedings 18th IEEE International Conference on Automated Software Engineering (ASE)* (2003), IEEE Computer Society, pp. 30–39.

[87] REPS, T., BALL, T., DAS, M., AND LARUS, J. The Use of Program Profiling for Software Maintenance with Applications to the Year 2000 Problem. In *Proceedings of the Sixth European Software Engineering Conference (ESEC/FSE 97)* (Sept. 1997), M. Jazayeri and H. Schauer, Eds., Lecture Notes in Computer Science Nr. 1013, Springer–Verlag, pp. 432–449.

[88] RINARD, M., CADAR, C., DUMITRAN, D., ROY, D. M., AND LEU, T. A Dynamic Technique for Eliminating Buffer Overflow Vulnerabilities (and Other Memory Errors). In *ACSAC '04: Proceedings of the 20th Annual Computer Security Applications Conference* (Washington, DC, USA, 2004), IEEE Computer Society, pp. 82–90.

[89] ROTHERMEL, G., AND HARROLD, M. J. Empirical Studies of a Safe Regression Test Selection Technique. *IEEE Transactions Software Engineering 24*, 6 (1998), 401–419.

[90] ROUNTEV, A. Precise Identification of Side-Effect-Free Methods in Java. In *ICSM '04: Proceedings of the 20th IEEE International Conference on Software Maintenance* (2004), IEEE Computer Society, pp. 82–91.

[91] RUTAR, N., ALMAZAN, C. B., AND FOSTER, J. S. A Comparison of Bug Finding Tools for Java. In *ISSRE '04: Proceedings of the 15th International Symposium on Software Reliability Engineering (ISSRE'04)* (Washington, DC, USA, 2004), IEEE Computer Society, pp. 245–256.

[92] SANTELICES, R., JONES, J. A., YANBING, Y., AND HARROLD, M. J. Lightweight Fault-localization Using Multiple Coverage Types. In *ICSE '09: Proceedings of the 2009 IEEE 31st International Conference on Software Engineering* (Washington, DC, USA, 2009), IEEE Computer Society, pp. 56–66.

[93] SCHULER, D., DALLMEIER, V., AND ZELLER, A. Efficient Mutation Testing by Checking Invariant Violations. In *ISSTA '09: Proceedings of the eighteenth International Symposium on Software Testing and Analysis* (New York, NY, USA, 2009), ACM, pp. 69–80.

[94] SHOHAM, S., YAHAV, E., FINK, S., AND PISTOIA, M. Static Specification Mining using Automata-based Abstractions. In *ISSTA '07: Proceedings of the 2007 International Symposium on Software Testing and Analysis* (New York, NY, USA, 2007), ACM, pp. 174–184.

[95] ŚLIWERSKI, J., ZIMMERMANN, T., AND ZELLER, A. When Do Changes Induce Fixes? On Fridays. In *Proceedings International Workshop on Mining Software Repositories (MSR)* (St. Louis, Missouri, U.S., May 2005).

[96] SPACCO, J., HOVEMEYER, D., AND PUGH, W. BugBench: Benchmarks for Evaluating Bug Detection Tools. In *PLDI Workshop on the Evaluation of Software Defect Detection Tools* (June 2005).

[97] SPACCO, J., STRECKER, J., HOVEMEYER, D., AND PUGH, W. Software Repository Mining with Marmoset: An Automated Programming Project Snapshot and Testing System. In *MSR '05: Proceedings of the 2005 International Workshop on Mining Software repositories* (New York, NY, USA, 2005), ACM Press, pp. 1–5. See also: http://marmoset.cs.umd.edu/.

[98] SRIDHARAN, M., AND BODÍK, R. Refinement-based Context-sensitive Points-to Analysis for Java. *SIGPLAN Notes 41*, 6 (2006), 387–400.

[99] STROM, R. E., AND YEMINI, S. Typestate: A programming Language Concept for Enhancing software Reliability. *Transactions Software Engineering 12*, 1 (1986), 157–171.

[100] SU, Z., AND MISHERGHI, G. HDD: Hierarchical Delta Debugging. *Software Engineering, International Conference on 0* (2006), 142–151.

[101] SĂLCIANU, A., AND RINARD, M. C. Purity and Side-effect Analysis for Java Programs. In *Proceedings of the 6th International Conference on Verification, Model Checking and Abstract Interpretation (VMCAI'05)* (2005), pp. 199–215.

[102] THIELE, M. Classification of Software Defects. Bachelor's thesis, Saarland University, January 2007.

[103] TONELLA, P. Evolutionary Testing of Classes. *SIGSOFT Software Engineering Notes 29*, 4 (2004), 119–128.

[104] VEANES, M., CAMPBELL, C., SCHULTE, W., AND TILLMANN, N. Online testing with Model Programs. *SIGSOFT Software Engineering Notes 30*, 5 (2005), 273–282.

[105] WASYLKOWSKI, A., ZELLER, A., AND LINDIG, C. Detecting Object Usage Anomalies. In *ESEC-FSE '07: Proceedings of the the 6th Joint Meeting of the European Software Engineering Conference and the ACM SIGSOFT Symposium on the Foundations of Software Engineering* (New York, NY, USA, 2007), ACM, pp. 35–44.

[106] WEIMER, W. Patches as Better Bug Reports. In *GPCE '06: Proceedings of the 5th International Conference on Generative Programming and component Engineering* (New York, NY, USA, 2006), ACM, pp. 181–190.

[107] WEIMER, W., NGUYEN, T., GOUES, C. L., AND FORREST, S. Automatically Finding Patches Using Genetic Programming. In *Proceedings of the International Conference on Software Engineering (ICSE)* (Vancouver, Canada, May 2009).

[108] WHALEY, J., MARTIN, M. C., AND LAM, M. S. Automatic Extraction of Object-oriented Component Interfaces. In *ISSTA '02: Proceedings of the 2002 ACM SIGSOFT International Symposium on Software Testing and Analysis* (New York, NY, USA, 2002), ACM, pp. 218–228.

[109] WHITTAKER, J. A., REKAB, K., AND THOMASON, M. G. A Markov Chain Model for Predicting the Reliability of Multi-build Software. *Information and Software Technology 42*, 12 (2000), 889 – 894.

[110] WILLIAMS, C., AND HOLLINGSWORTH, J. K. Bug Driven Bug Finders. In *Proceedings International Workshop on Mining Software Repositories (MSR 2004)* (Edinburgh, Scotland, UK, May 2004), pp. 70–74.

[111] WILLIAMS, C. C., AND HOLLINGSWORTH, J. K. Automatic Mining of Source Code Repositories to Improve Bug Finding Techniques. *IEEE Transactions on Software Engineering 31*, 6 (2005), 466–480.

[112] WORLD WIDE WEB CONSORTIUM. "XML Path Language (XPath)". http://www.w3c.org/TR/xpath/.

[113] XIE, T., MARTIN, E., AND YUAN, H. Automatic Extraction of Abstract-object-state Machines from Unit-test Executions. In *ICSE '06: Proceedings of the 28th International Conference on Software Engineering* (New York, NY, USA, 2006), ACM, pp. 835–838.

[114] XIE, T., AND NOTKIN, D. Mutually Enhancing Test Generation and Specification Inference. In *Proceedings of the 3rd International Workshop on Formal Approaches to Testing of Software (FATES 03)* (October 2003), vol. 2931 of *LNCS*, pp. 60–69.

[115] XIE, Y., AND ENGLER, D. Using Redundancies to Find Errors. *IEEE Transactions on Software Engineering 29*, 10 (2003), 915–928.

[116] XU, H., PICKETT, C. J. F., AND VERBRUGGE, C. Dynamic Purity Analysis for Java Programs. In *Proceedings of the 7th Workshop on Program Analysis for Software Tools and Engineering* (2007), ACM, pp. 75–82.

[117] YANG, J., EVANS, D., BHARDWAJ, D., BHAT, T., AND DAS, M. Perracotta: Mining Temporal API Rules from Imperfect Traces. In *ICSE '06: Proceeding of the 28th International Conference on Software Engineering* (New York, NY, USA, 2006), ACM Press, pp. 282–291.

[118] ZELLER, A. Yesterday, My Program Worked. Today, it does Not. Why? In *Proceedings of the ESEC/FSE'99, 7th European Software Engineering Conference* (September 1999), vol. 1687 of *Lecture Notes in Computer Science*, Springer, pp. 253–267.

[119] ZELLER, A. *Why Programs Fail: A Guide to Systematic Debugging.* Morgan Kaufmann Publishers Inc., San Francisco, CA, USA, 2009.

[120] ZELLER, A., AND HILDEBRANDT, R. Simplifying and Isolating Failure-Inducing Input. *IEEE Transactions on Software Engineering 28*, 2 (February 2002), 183–200.

[121] ZHANG, X., GUPTA, N., AND GUPTA, R. Locating Faults Through Automated Predicate Switching. In *ICSE '06: Proceeding of the 28th International Conference on Software Engineering* (New York, NY, USA, 2006), ACM Press, pp. 272–281.

[122] ZIMMERMANN, T. Fine-grained Processing of CVS Archives with APFEL. In *Proceedings of the 2006 OOPSLA Workshop on Eclipse Technology eXchange* (New York, NY, USA, October 2006), ACM Press.

[123] ZIMMERMANN, T., DALLMEIER, V., HALACHEV, K., AND ZELLER, A. eROSE: Guiding Programmers in Eclipse (Tool Demonstration). In *Companion to the 20th Annual ACM SIGPLAN Conference on Object-Oriented Programming, Systems, Languages, and Applications, OOPSLA 2005* (New York, NY, USA, October 2005), ACM, pp. 186–187.

[124] ZIMMERMANN, T., PREMRAJ, R., AND ZELLER, A. Predicting Defects for Eclipse. In *Proceedings of the Third International Workshop on Predictor Models in Software Engineering* (May 2007).

[125] ZIMMERMANN, T., AND WEISSGERBER, P. Preprocessing CVS Data for Fine-Grained Analysis. In *Proceedings of International Workshop on Mining Software Repositories (MSR 2004)* (Edinburgh, Scotland, UK, May 2004), pp. 2–6.

Die VDM Verlagsservicegesellschaft sucht für wissenschaftliche Verlage abgeschlossene und herausragende

Dissertationen, Habilitationen, Diplomarbeiten, Master Theses, Magisterarbeiten usw.

für die kostenlose Publikation als Fachbuch.

Sie verfügen über eine Arbeit, die hohen inhaltlichen und formalen Ansprüchen genügt, und haben Interesse an einer honorarvergüteten Publikation?

Dann senden Sie bitte erste Informationen über sich und Ihre Arbeit per Email an *info@vdm-vsg.de*.

Sie erhalten kurzfristig unser Feedback!

VDM Verlagsservicegesellschaft mbH
Dudweiler Landstr. 99
D - 66123 Saarbrücken

Telefon +49 681 3720 174
Fax   +49 681 3720 1749

www.vdm-vsg.de

Die VDM Verlagsservicegesellschaft mbH vertritt

Printed by Books on Demand GmbH, Norderstedt / Germany